The Universal Call

A Journey to Consciousness

Fatima El-Hindi

DEDICATION

This book is dedicated to the loving memory of my parents Mohamad Tahar Meghezzi and Fella Barkat. They have served as an inspiration for this book. I would like to thank all those who assisted and contributed to the writing of the book, and my friends and family who have worked with me at Nas Learning Center and were instrumental in its growth and success. There are so many that it is not feasible to mention each by name. I also thank my husband Lawrence and my children, and express gratitude to my husband's parents, Ahmad and Elizabeth El-Hindi, who have long supported and helped us.

Special thanks to my friend Kussay Hashem Fakhir for his steadfast collegiality, and for suggesting I write about my journey to help others with their own. Also special thanks to Daniel Shortell, who edited the book, and Emily Pollokoff, who was my right hand in its creation. Without their consistent review and patience with me, this book would not be done.

CONTENTS

ACKNOWLEDGMENTS

I would like to express my appreciation for my students and their willingness to share their stories and contribute to this book. Again, the purpose for their inclusion into the book is not for my self-promotion, but to give my students an opportunity to share their personal experiences and journeys and their evolution to a greater truth, a higher level of consciousness through their own self-realization and intellect. We offer their stories to motivate others to open their minds and doors to a novel understanding of the universal call.

FOREWORD

I have always known Fatima as a whirlwind. She always has projects going, both new ideas to pursue and old projects to improve. You never really know what you are going to get done when you sit down for a meeting with her. Sometimes, you have a mission and see it through to the end right then and there. And sometimes, inspiration surges and changes the plan. Whatever happens, you know you are going to experience an authentic interaction.

These days, it is not so easy to encounter people who are 110% comfortable with who they are and their role in the universe. People tend to waste a lot of time tiptoeing around big questions, unwilling to face the consequences of their own humanity. Fatima, though, is clear about her purpose, rightfully unapologetic for her impressive skill set, and equally as humble about her shortcomings (few though one may perceive them to be). From my perspective as her student, employee, and co-worker--I can indeed use both the latter terms, having experienced both her confident leadership and her insistence on mutually respectful, collaborative process--I know that what you see is what you get.

Or is it? In a way, you are getting a lot more than what you can see. Fatima brings her lifetime of experience to every moment. Her hardships have been many, and are treated only lightly (!) in the following pages. This is partly to protect her privacy, and partly because, as she will be the first to tell you, it does not matter so much what you go through, as how you approached the challenge and what you took away from it. What may be a trifling matter for one person can be earth-shattering for another. How we grow as people is not defined by what obstacles we face, but in how we come away with them, whether tail tucked and shoulders slumped, or looking ahead bravely to new possibilities.

I hope that the wisdom Fatima shares in this volume will help you find new ways to affirm your value as a person, so you too can learn how to face your life with courage and hope despite any odds. When I met Fatima, my life was not in a good place, and the guidance she offered was instrumental in helping me move on from that situation. If Fatima strives to live by example, I could not have asked for a more timely or appropriate role-model. Our lives had taken some of the same turns, and her mature perspective was just what I needed to get a grip, make better choices, and maintain a more optimistic outlook despite the tremendous difficulty I felt I was experiencing at the time.

From my perspective as an American "Muslim" who rejects many aspects of traditional Islamic practice (hence the quotes), it is also refreshing to hear someone speak about the Qur'an in such a clear and timeless way. What first drew me to the Qur'an was its egalitarian (if not feminist) and logical attitude towards the nature of the soul, its elegant explanation of the individual's relationship to the cosmos, and its strong emphasis of the miracle of existence in all its infinite beauty. In discussing Fatima's work with her, I feel like someone has finally gained the courage to break with convention and boldly reclaim this incredible text from the clutches of history. Fatima's linguistic approach makes new connections unavailable in other literature. By extracting original meaning as best one can in another language, Fatima makes this ancient Arabic text relevant and fresh for contemporary English readers.

I believe that just like the messages revealed in the Qur'an, Fatima's teachings will also endure in value. I invite you to set aside any preconceived notions about Islam, Muslims, and the Qur'an whether as a holy scripture or historical text, and consider merely that she offers some interesting personal guidance using her background as an incidental frame of reference. There are many places in this book where you will feel invited to explore how her ideas are applicable to your own life and experiences. At this time, ask yourself, how can you deploy the powerful sum of your knowledge to not just understand where you are, but to propel yourself where you want to be? If her ideas are new to you, try applying them. If they resonate--and I think many of them will, as they did with me--then I encourage you to go deeper into your own spiritual practices. Really reconnect with your Source, and yourself. Do what you need to do for your soul to become its own best possible version. How can this not be worth the effort?

I wish you a pleasant journey around the castle of your being. You may wander down hallways you would prefer to leave behind, open doors that you will happily and quickly close again. But you may also discover new passageways to realms you thought surely inaccessible. If we are all indeed reflections of the Infinite, then there is no small treasure in your heart. It is time to let it shine!

~Emily Pollokoff

1

MY JOURNEY TO NLC

I have always loved cats. My first cat's name was Namira. I recall one day when I was six years old and she was wandering around, meowing in pain. I asked my mom what was wrong and she replied that Namira's cries were natural, as she was in labor, and that soon she would have a few kittens. I spent the entire night watching her deliver four healthy kittens. As she cared for them, I wondered how the kittens were not injured whenever Namira carried them in her mouth. Who or what was guiding her to do what she was doing if she was not human, like us, using her intellect? My questions about the cat became deeper and deeper ones about myself: who am I? What is my purpose? Where do we go when we die? My family responded to these queries by merely repeating the common answers circulating in our society, but these did not satisfy me.

I began reading every book I could find in the library about self-awareness, religion, God, and science. I read books written for adults as children's books did not quench my curiosity or answer my questions. Being raised in Algeria in a bilingual environment embracing multiple cultures—primarily French, Arabic, and Turkish—I was exposed at an early age to diverse thinking and open-mindedness. Even though I came from a Muslim family, I gave equal opportunity to Muslim and non-Muslim authors in both Arabic and French literature. It would be many years, however, before I realized that the answers I was seeking were already available to me and were as ubiquitous as the air I breathed. The answers sought trickled in over time, and were revealed by simply going through the process of life itself.

Learning how to access this information took me down a convoluted path. My dream as a teenager was to study math in America, and this dream intensified when my uncle got his scholarship to study at Syracuse University (SU) in New York. Within two years, he arranged for me to follow him there through an arranged marriage with his friend. The driving force for me to get married was that it provided a means to escape some of the cultural and traditional forms of Islam which I began to question at a young age. When I challenged my teachers and elders about certain rules and regulations of Islamic society (especially those concerning women's rights), I could not find answers that made sense to me and the answers I did find contradicted not only the text of the Qur'an but also basic human logic. For example, the interpretation of qur'anic verse 4:34 in the opinion of most Islamic jurists is that a man has the right to beat a woman if she is disobedient. This never made sense to me as it was not congruent with the principles of justice and basic human rights that were given to humans by an authority higher than "man." Additionally, in many traditional quranic interpretations, women are required to have a related male chaperone, be he a husband, father, or brother, in order to access certain "freedoms," such as travel. In my own case, culturally, I could not travel and study in another land without living with my family or a spouse, hence the marriage setup I faced as I traveled west.

I still recall landing at JFK, alone at age 18, looking around for the future husband I was about to meet for the first time. Although deep down in my heart I feared the unknown, I also had hope in the greater forces of the universe. This hope is what sustained me through the tumult of the next eleven years. And of course, these trials all informed my perspective on the nature of life itself, and the questions I had began pondering after the birth of Namira's kittens.

As it turned out, I was unable to attend SU as expected. It turned out that my husband was an Algerian-born imam himself, completely immersed in the religious and cultural dogma I thought I had left behind at home. His thoughts did not align with my understanding of the universal structure and orientation of Islam, and it was out of the question for him for me to attend school. After the births of two sons, one of the biggest problems in our marriage became a differing viewpoint on how to function as a family, a problem rooted in our differences in Islamic understanding. This problem is what led me to decide to terminate the marriage by asking for a divorce. I realized that I could not live in harmony with the universe if the basic aspects of my daily life resulted in constant argument.

After my divorce, I took full custody of my boys and sought support from my family. I decided to stay with my parents back in Algeria to pursue my college education. They were supportive, but worried about my future. Indeed, it must have been concerning to them, but all I could feel was contentment that I had taken control of my life and was enjoying a renewed opportunity to pursue my dreams. The day I received my divorce letter, I zoomed into the family room and announced, "I got my freedom back, congratulate me!" My mother looked up from television in tears, and reminded me of the difficulties I would face raising two boys as a divorcee. I paused to consider her perspective and felt a rush of intuition. After a moment, I answered her, "I'm not worried. I will focus on my degree and then go back to the US, get my PhD, and marry a man who understands me and will always be willing to stand by me. Then, I will have a daughter as a first child with my new husband." The utterance was part prayer (a hope of what might be) and part prediction (confidently seeing what will be). This appeal to The Source did not go unanswered.

After four years of extensive work at Constantine University in Algeria, I received a scholarship from SU to its PhD program in mechanical engineering, achieving my first goal. Within the first month of my return to New York I met my current husband, Lawrence, a man who has been a huge support in my journey of learning. Although he is a Palestinian-American raised by his Lebanese-Catholic mom, we have never had an intercultural conflict in our twenty-plus years together. Our marriage marked the completion of the second goal. Sure enough, shortly after our marriage, we were blessed with our first child, a daughter, rounding out my third goal uttered in a prayer only a few years prior. How could I be anything but grateful?

Despite our happiness, however, life's challenges kept multiplying, as they do. I had been forced to leave my two young boys with my parents until I settled at SU again, and a slew of immigration issues further prevented me from bringing my boys to the U.S. even after getting myself settled. Ultimately, it took three-and-a-half years to reunite with my sons, who were only five and seven years old when I left for the U.S. the second time! Looking back, I am certain I only made it through the difficulties of separation by focusing like a laser on my PhD studies, and concentrating my heart on the gratitude I felt for the many blessings I did have in my life. The separation from my children was the biggest challenge of my life. Nevertheless, this formative experience steeled me for every challenge I have faced since then.

My boys and I finally reunited when my daughter was seven months old. I was very grateful to have my family together after such a long separation. A short while afterwards, my mother visited us in the U.S. as she desperately missed the boys she had raised for so long. During her visit she recalled, in amused shock, what I had told her many years earlier, after my divorce. As we discussed the uncanny alignment between the milestones of my life and the intuitive statement I made previously, it became crystal clear to me what efforts I had taken to essentially bootstrap success and doggedly push toward the end result I had seen in my mind years earlier. However, regardless of the challenging efforts required to persevere, I always did my best to maintain a perpetual song of thanks in my heart. These feelings of gratitude seemed vital to me, and like something that helped realize my successes.

Coincidentally, at the end of that summer in 1998, my husband was relocated to Arizona for his work and we settled in the town of Chandler, a growing suburb of Phoenix. We have warm memories of the six years we spent there, and are grateful to our friends from that time, but our family challenges did not cease. For example, we had no family to help us with our young children. As such, when I went into labor with my second daughter in the middle of the night, we simply woke up our boys (then 10 and 12), reminded them to watch over their two-year-old sister, and headed to the hospital. Within minutes of the delivery, I sent Lawrence home to get the boys ready for school and take care of our daughter.

When this baby was old enough for daycare, I returned to teaching mathematics at Maricopa

Community College. My husband's work as a Field and Sales Engineer required him to travel away from home often, sometimes for weeks at a time. Imagine the challenge of dealing with adolescent boys and young children at the same time, with their different interests and psychological needs. The boys were still adjusting to life and culture in the US, which was so different from their native Algeria. I was younger then, but it was exhausting to be driving to and from work, and taking the kids to and from daycare, not to mention giving rides to the older kids for school. On top of that were the duties of maintaining the house, fetching groceries, and tending to all the needs of the household. It was a life so far removed from the circumstances I grew up with in Algeria, where family and extended family helped each other like a village.

Life became even more challenging when I was expecting the birth of my fifth child. In the late spring of 2001 we got word from Algeria that my father had fallen ill. The doctors suspected cancer of the pancreas and liver. My father had to travel from Algeria to the U.S. for treatment at Upstate University Hospital in Syracuse, where my siblings were living at the time. Lawrence and I traveled back to Syracuse that summer to reunite with my father and family. We found out that my father's cancer had metastasized and the doctors estimated that he had only a few months or perhaps a year to live. I could not stay long in New York because I was nearing my delivery date and could not delay the return to Arizona, so I had to say goodbye to him in the hospital. I told my father that I would return after the baby was born, but deep in my heart I knew I was saying goodbye to him for the last time. My father died in the hospital just a couple weeks before our son was born in August 2001, just one month before the horrific 9/11 attacks on the United States.

The events of September 11 came to be one of the significant experiences of our time in Arizona. On that same day, my husband had left early that morning to catch a flight for business travel. The older boys were already in school. As the morning's events unfolded on live TV, everything stopped. We were glued to the TV and witnessed a national human tragedy. There were feelings of shock, disbelief, and outrage. As a Muslim American it became instantly concerning because the events were already being tied to al-Qaeda and "Islamic Terror." At the same time, Lawrence called me to say that all flights were canceled and he was already returning from the airport. I told him to go directly to the school to pick up the boys because, as visibly two of the very few Muslims in the entire school system, I was afraid that they could be harassed or bullied for what other Muslims had done.

As the day drew to a close there was much feeling of loss and anxiety. We had feared that the events would result in harassment and alienation of the Muslim community. That evening, as we saw the smoke emanating from the Manhattan Skyline on CNN, we felt an atmosphere of depression but also inevitable anxiety and fear of impending hostility toward those of the Islamic faith. My husband reminded me that my U.S. Citizenship Naturalization Ceremony was scheduled for the end of the month. Would it be safe to attend the ceremony? In the days to come we saw that people summoned their better selves. Many friends and strangers reached out to show their support. It was heartwarming to see people of other faiths hold protective vigils outside the local Islamic centers. Weeks later when my husband and I attended the Naturalization Ceremony in downtown Phoenix with our youngest in the baby carrier and myself in Islamic dress (hijab), everyone greeted us warmly. We witnessed in those weeks and the next few years that there are universal and natural feelings of support and compassion among people, and a respect for fairness and justice. We definitely benefited spiritually from this tough period of learning and growth, and today it is easier to feel thankful for these challenges we faced together.

We resettled in Syracuse in spring 2004. This meant readjusting to the community we had left, and of course, changing schools for all the kids. It was interesting to witness our adjustments in lifestyle and family culture as we moved from a sprawling and developing suburb full of recent transplants, to a comparatively more rural environment, where the physical and social landscape did not change much from generation to generation. Integrating among families who had comprised the local social fabric for scores of years inspired us to put down our roots here, too, and eventually propelled our family on a new venture in serving the community.

But what would making dreams come true mean without a few more "small" surprises to face, first? I met my husband at the door when he returned from work on a summer afternoon in 2004, and told him, "I have some news for you that you won't believe," with a hint of exasperation in my voice. He replied, eyes strained, in a tone of disbelief, "Don't tell me. One of the boys got in trouble. What is it? Did someone get pregnant?" I was annoyed that he could think such a thing of the boys I had been raising with such care, and replied curtly, "No, it's you. It's what you did. I am pregnant again!" With my oldest in college, I thought I was finished changing diapers, but here we were, expanding our family for the final time. Our sixth child was born in mid-February. As we bundled him up in hats and cozy socks, we laughed at the extreme contrast with the birth of his older brother, who was born in the August heat of Arizona just a few years earlier. I might not have planned to change more diapers until grandmotherhood, but our youngest was an unexpected blessing.

Soon after, catastrophe punctuated our life, and changed my professional trajectory forever. My mother of sixty-three years was visiting, staying with the family in Syracuse upon the completion of her pilgrimage to Mecca. She was anxious to get back to her home in Algeria. Days before she left with my husband, who was driving her to JFK airport that blustery January morning, I had a vision or premonition of impending loss. I had the feeling that I would be saying goodbye to her for the last time. Later that afternoon, Lawrence called me from JFK airport. He calmly informed me that they had arrived and were waiting for the check-in counter to open. I asked to speak with my mother and he told me that she just went to wash and pray, as Royal Air Maroc Airlines had a small prayer area adjacent to the ticketing and check-in counter. Just a few minutes later, I answered the phone to Lawrence calling out in a frantic and panicked voice, "Your mother just collapsed after praying. She is unconscious. The medics are here and asking about her medications. We are taking her to the hospital. Pray for her. I'll call you back!" With that, I knew we had lost her. I told my son right away, "Get the house ready. People are coming. Hajja is dead."

It was in those days we felt most keenly the power and wisdom of the universe. My father had passed away just five years earlier and although he lived all his life in Algeria, he was buried where he died, in Syracuse. Our mother fully intended to return to Algeria to live out her days. She felt that this would be her last trip to the U.S. due to her health conditions of high-blood pressure and diabetes. Instead, her end-of-life journey brought her back to Syracuse by way of the Brooklyn funeral home van. Her funeral and burial place were situated just yards away from my father's plot at Oakwood Cemetery. Ironically, they would share the same resting place, but in a land thousands of miles and an ocean away from their homeland.

Our mother was never formally educated, but she had wisdom that we could never replace. She had raised nine children and helped raise grandchildren, too, while always helping my father who had lost one of his arms in an industrial accident when he was just a teenager. She supported him as he built his furniture business from nothing in Algeria. He himself grew up in poverty and was orphaned as a child, and had to work on the streets as a young boy to help support his mother and siblings. Hajja, as we called her, always emphasized hard work, orderliness, cleanliness, and doing well in school. Even though she was illiterate herself, she pushed all of us, including the five sisters, to pursue an education. We would be amused when she would push us to read and study while holding our open books upside down. Being illiterate, she did not know the right side of the page. We deeply felt her sudden loss and grieved that we did not thank her and my father enough for their sacrifices and support for the family and the community.

My mother's nickname, Hajja, was typically reserved for those who had performed the hajj (ritual pilgrimage to Mecca), but could also be reverently used for someone who has experienced a pilgrimage through life and learned many lessons from life's victories and hardships. In our mother's time and before hers, I believe there was more respect for the wisdom and honor of motherhood, and a mother's important guidance for the family and society. It seems that in our generation, or "modern times," this respect and sense of appreciation has eroded. Today there is more value in textbook or "traditional" institutionalized learning, which over the years has by and large been written by men, and does not universally appreciate the value of women and mothers in society. But what of the practice and spiritual wisdom that had earned my mother such a respected moniker?

I felt that as I was approaching middle-age and benefiting from my mother's wisdom and the wealth of knowledge from my own life's journey that there is a knowledge base that cannot be matched by a scholastic or collegiate curriculum. Whether we study to be a doctor, a lawyer, a scientist, journalist, engineer, artist or business practitioner we must benefit from the wisdom gained from our journey and the journey of others and appreciate the value of it. The greatest wisdom is the knowledge of character and the correct way to deal with others in interpersonal relationships whether it is family members, spouses, friends, the workplace, or the social community. This is perhaps part of emotional intelligence. Although we are in an age where higher education is very accessible and in-demand (albeit expensive and incurring financial debt in many cases), we are lacking the fundamental knowledge or wisdom that does not have a price tag. Without this wisdom, we lack the consciousness of who we are, why are we here, what is our purpose? Although my mother was never formally educated, she performed a lifetime pilgrimage to wisdom and consciousness. She is an example of the many people I draw inspiration from and a figure who motivates me to continue my own journey toward wisdom and consciousness. We cannot forget that such journeys are not without struggle alongside reward, and that the balance of struggle and reward is not equal for everyone.

After my mother's passing, I started having intense feelings about sharing my experiences, using them as a tool to help educate and empower women and young adults in my community. I had this notion that I wanted to help others strive toward their dreams regardless of the obstacles encountered. A constant voice in my head told me that humans were not destined to be lazy, greedy creatures, but rather we were created to find success by practicing gratitude with a sense of joy. It was then that I began a life-long project of giving back.

In 2006, I founded a weekend school program at a local mosque to teach the Arabic language as well as Islamic art, history and civilization. The idea was to provide students with a rich and encompassing understanding of what it means to be Muslim, to go beyond the typical education provided in a mosque. Being new to the community, I brought an outsider's perspective and realized the school needed a foundational rework in all aspects: curriculum, scheduling, and the process of purchasing school supplies, equipment, and learning materials. It was challenging to lead this effort whilst simultaneously caring for my six children, one of whom was only a year old at the time. However, the most difficult task I faced was navigating the politics and bureaucracy established by the community leaders and embedded in their educational paradigm. I realized that the biggest obstacle to the program's success was not the structure I planned for the school, but rather, the cultural "baggage" many of the community leaders brought with them from their native countries, baggage that prevented them from thinking beyond their formal, traditional perspectives. I felt that this cultural inflexibility was detrimental to the creation of an honest and truthful Islamic educational program, so I parted ways with the mosque in order to keep true to my ideals and beliefs.

This departure led me and other members of the community to start our own independent Sunday school, Nas Learning Center (NLC). The name includes the Arabic word nās, meaning "people," to indicate a place where all people can gather to learn from each other about our collective experience on Earth. Although we continue to teach the Arabic language and the history and culture of Islam to this day, our pedagogy hinges on developing self-awareness within an Islamic context. As such, the Qur'an, being the sole universally legitimate text of Muslims worldwide, is used as a beacon to help illuminate the path to self-awareness. Our belief is that the Qur'an is not simply a set of verses to be memorized nor a list of laws to be followed; rather, it is an incredible collection of universal truths that, when distilled from their social and historical context, provide flawless insights into the human condition that can be leveraged to assist with daily life. Developing the indispensable critical thinking skills necessary to extract the truths from the Qur'an is vital to preparing Muslim youth for full engagement in our multicultural, diverse society. The goal of Nas Learning Center is to help students learn and live by good values, and respect the laws of human behaviour by being just, respectful, and compassionate. Our "Islamic studies" classes emphasize critical thinking about source texts, rather than defaulting to the methodology and structure of the traditional schools, which have emphasized rote memorization of scripture and relied on centuries-old translations, and historical facts of questionable basis. We want to give our students the valuable powers of analysis, so they will be equipped with proper tools with which to dissect the meaning of the language of the Qur'an.

Why the Qur'an, though? If our guiding principles are so "universal," why establish our center in a faith-specific context? I will put it this way. In 2019 I had the opportunity to attend a "Celebrate Your Life" retreat in Sedona, AZ where I met developmental biologist and spiritual scientist Dr. Bruce Lipton. In conversation with Dr. Lipton, he compared religions to individually decorated, but otherwise identical Christmas trees. Everyone decorates a Christmas tree in their own way, Lipton explained, but the physical tree is basically the same for everyone. If we look past the different decorations, we can see that the Truths are constant and steadfast. I mention Lipton's perspective to explain that while I reference the Qur'an throughout this book, and its teachings flow as the undercurrent of my life, this is simply because it is the set of ornaments I know best. I am fully aware that the beautiful truths of existence are contained within all ancient religious scriptures. Much like Islam, the universal truths of these texts are also subject to elimination or obfuscation by scholarly opinion, bias and/or cultural control, but I will leave it to experts in other fields to attempt their clarification. So, given my own background, I can confidently draw only upon the Qur'an in my work for the sake of raising collective consciousness.

Part of what reinforces my commitment to using the Qur'an as a tool to explain issues of consciousness to both "Muslims" and "non-Muslims" is that once the cultural scaffolding and traditional scholarly interpretations are disassembled and removed, we are left with a text that speaks broadly to universal issues--and, there do exist immutable truths here on Earth, and nobody, regardless of their status, wealth, or power has the ability to circumvent the universal laws that govern human existence. For example, there are basic biological laws that are inescapable for all humans. All humans and living things are subject to the physical laws of the universe such as gravity, birth, death and the basic human reality of existing and being physically present for their journey on planet Earth. All humans and living beings must have water and air to survive. Regardless of how an individual worships (or does not), we all must submit to the physical laws that establish the operating environment for living beings. In a similar vein, there are also "social laws" embedded in the universal human experience that, while not inescapable like the physical laws, are universal and innately demanded by humans regardless of culture. These "social laws" include certain inviolable human rights, systems of justice, and principles of fairness.

When pondering the universality of the Qur'an, verse 3:83 always comes to mind. It says, "Do they desire other than the universal laws of God, when to Him has submitted everything in the heavens and the earth, willingly or unwillingly, and to Him they will be returned?" In other words, considering that certain truths of the human experience are universally valid, if we posit that "God" and the "universal laws" are one unified concept, then does it not follow that all humans are subject to them? In this sense, drawing on the Arabic definition of "Muslim" as "one who submits," if we can say that all people existing on Earth must submit to the exact same universal laws, then all humans are inherently "Muslim" regardless of what they believe or which God they choose to worship (or not). This is not to say that all people know about the Qur'an or have an understanding of the history of Islam as a human institution. Rather, it is to say that all people can benefit from the lessons offered by the Qur'an, a text "for Muslims," which can also be seen as a universal text, because it describes universal truths from which humans are incapable of altering or escaping.

So the question arises, if the message of the Qur'an is truly universal, then why is it uncommon to hear Islamic scholars and imams communicate the message of the Qur'an in this broad manner? And why are most Muslims held captive by ancient, culturally-specific interpretations of a text that speaks to the basic human condition? Why has the message of the Qur'an become so politicized and divergent across the various cultures of the Muslim world? Broad analytical research done over many years has led me to find many poor interpretations of the Qur'an that are not only misleading but in fact skew the universal intent of the original Arabic text. This research has helped to refine my understanding of Islam. And of course, it has strengthened my commitment to using a pure linguistic approach to analyzing the Qur'an, to better extract the universally applicable wisdom contained therein.

This book draws on some of the guiding lessons from both my life experiences and my analytical research of the Qur'an. My hope is that the stories, anecdotes, and analysis contained within will help empower people going through difficulties regardless of their belief system (or lack thereof). Having endured tribulation myself, and having survived deep grief and searing anguish, I feel an obligation to share the perspectives that have helped me through my challenging days. I strongly believe that my calling in life is to leverage my experiences and my understanding of the Qur'an to explain to the world that happiness and peace are within everyone's grasp, no matter the circumstances. Spoiler alert: the Universal Call is to love and coexistence.

But how do we get there? Discussing this journey is now the task at hand. The first step toward this beautiful destination is establishing a mindset of gratitude.

2

THE RIGHT STATE OF MIND

The first rule of a gratitude mindset is that it must persist through thick and thin. After all, life is full of ups and downs, but we can always be grateful for our blessings throughout the difficult times as well as the easy days. Adopting this perspective can bring unimaginable rewards. Maintaining a positive state of mind during one of the most negative periods in my own life even allowed me to experience a miracle first-hand.

The years of separation from my boys were incredibly difficult. I missed them so much, and back then communication technologies were limited. We did not have FaceTime or other video conferencing tools offering instant contact for free. One day I sat meditating before sunrise as I always do, and suddenly I envisioned my mother taking my second son to the hospital. I called my mom to find out if there was any truth to this intuition. Sure enough, he had suffered a seizure. My heart could not stand it and I called daily during his recovery, talking for up to 30 minutes per call. It was very expensive to make a basic international phone call, about $3 per minute, but I could not resist, and I had already been calling my sons much more than was financially manageable. Dreading the bill at the end of month, I was shocked to see a balance due of $0.00. Where was the $2,000+ charge for which I had been pinching pennies? I called the phone company to verify the charges, but the representative assured me that their accounts showed no record of my daily check-ins with my boys. A true miracle.

How could I have been so lucky to receive such a blessing? I know that I am essentially no different than any other person. I am just as human, and perhaps more prone to illness. Like anyone, I am susceptible to feelings of anger, frustration and intemperance. On the surface, nothing could distinguish me as extra eligible for divine favor. Success against great odds, however, is directly related to the internal efforts one makes to connect with the ultimate goodness of the universal consciousness. Gratitude is a primary method for making this connection.

When separated from and desperately missing my children, I realized I had the choice to let my mentality succumb to my overwhelming feelings of impatience and powerlessness, or I could choose to concentrate on the many blessings in my life. After all, when we focus on our blessings, we attract more of them, as our increased concentration directs inordinate amounts of energy to the area of focus. A position of gratitude is, in large part, a matter of perception and awareness. In the Qur'an, verse 7:14 tells us, "and if you are grateful, I will increase your abundance." Over the years, this touchstone verse propelled me through difficult situations, and my uncanny experience with the phone company only strengthened my belief in its truth.

Years later, beyond the phone company incident, ideas about how the universe operated began to crystallize in my mind. Through reflection, I realized that there seemed to be a set of "ground rules" of mindset and behavior that carried me through other difficult situations in life. While waiting for my children's immigration issue to be resolved, I focused all of my energy on achieving my degree in mechanical engineering, and rededicating myself to living by these rules. To focus on the blessings. And indeed, by focusing on internal harmony during this time of external discord helped strengthen my spirit in every way. Focusing on the positive and establishing a deep sense of gratitude in the heart has been an underlying tenet that has sustained me throughout life.

Establish Gratitude

The foundational pillar of internal peace is gratitude. With thankfulness in the heart, every day is a blessing and a joy. That said, many challenges arise in life that aim to disrupt this idealistic perspective. Therefore, it is beneficial to develop a deliberate, daily practice of gratitude to serve as a ballast against the emotional ebbs and flows in life. Personally, I take advantage of the first moments after waking to meditate on being thankful for a new day and the many blessings in my life, no matter how simple. This time of focused reflection and the attention granted to the positive aspects of life helped me to sharpen my focus on my schoolwork and research whilst in university and it enabled me to excel academically. It also reset the compass of my heart to direct me forward into a good day.

If internal peace is a beautiful flower, gratitude is the water and fertilizer that helps it to grow. Throughout the day, seek more opportunities to water this plant. Enjoy the present moment when engaged in conversation or when simply in the company of others. Look outside for the natural entertainment of trees and little creatures going about their daily lives and marvel at their activity. One should read biographies of figures such as Muhammad al-Ghazali, and Joe Dispenza, as the both have excellent stories of how to foster an attitude of thankfulness and the positive impacts it had on their lives. Finally, encourage gratitude to expand and grow around you by practicing generosity and setting the example for how to outwardly express gratitude. The more you feed the flower of gratitude, the bigger and more beautiful it will grow in your heart and in the hearts of others.

Take Responsibility

"No one saves us but ourselves, no one can and no one may. We ourselves must walk the path." ~Buddha

People should try their best in everything they do and take charge of their life. To put this into practice, we need to take responsibility for our emotions, and focus on translating our feelings and desires into actions that positively impact the world around us. Engaging awareness of what is taking place in our mind is the first step. Many factors affect our consciousness, and not all of them for the better. Cultivating self-awareness through any number of strategies helps us avoid self-generated negativity, such as fear, anger, anxiety, and unhappiness. It has been well-documented in recent studies that negative mental stress can have negative effects on the body's immune system. Many health issues and illnesses such as heart disease, autoimmune diseases, and several gastrointestinal problems are known to be exacerbated by stress. If we allow negativity to destroy our minds and bodies, our spirits will also suffer.

Taking responsibility for our feelings will also help us be responsible for our actions, and guide ourselves towards making choices that have the greatest positive impact on the universe. We need to examine every decision we make by asking ourselves these questions: how will my choice help me grow, and how will my choice affect me and the people around me? When we consider the various moving parts at play in any scenario, we can best determine which course of action will lead us to the most comprehensive and inclusive measure of success. Considering the effects of our actions on the world outside of our own selves offers us the opportunity to grow to our fullest potential, because we maximize both our happiness and the happiness of the world around us. If the world around is happier, how can we not also become even happier, and thus more willing and able to further the cycle of improvement?

An important component of taking

responsibility for one's own actions is to remember that we are the masters of our own destinies. We do not need to say that our fate has already been "written" or pre-ordained whether good or bad. Of course, there may be events that happen out of our control, but it is how we deal with them and our attitude toward adversity that matters most. If we encounter a setback, then we should strive to maintain a positive attitude to the best of our ability. One technique for sustaining a positive state of mind in difficult situations is to imagine the possibility of a better outcome resulting from an apparent disaster. Should we not see one, or have difficulty imagining one, we can try to make physical efforts towards creating a better outcome. Failing all else, if we can simply trust that something good may potentially happen, we will open our hearts to gratitude, and to success.

Embrace Adversity with Patience

Coping with challenging situations, especially the ones that make us feel devoid of hope and lacking courage, presents a unique opportunity to develop a key quality that enhances a success mindset. Patience is the light that helps us see through the dark days of hardship. If we consider all the problems we face as a means of growth and evolution, then there is no need to resist or avoid the adversities that constantly aim to drag us down. Instead, we can welcome them into our lives, as they may help us learn. The problems lie not in the challenges we face but in how we choose to approach them.

If we accept that patience and perseverance are natural states of being, then we can feel more ready to consciously engage these qualities. After all, patience and perseverance are encoded in the law of nature. It takes nine months from conception to delivery in the human birth cycle, and it takes years for a seed that germinates in the soil to become a tree. Despite days of irregular nutrition or physical disturbance, the fetus and the seedling do not just "give up" in their journeys to becoming their greatest selves. So too must we commit our fledgling souls to pushing forward in our growth.

Even accidentally self-inflicted adversity and

failure have their benefits. The word "failure" in our society has negative connotations. This viewpoint is shortsighted, however, as many successful people know all too well: we learn and grow from failure. History is full of stories of artists, athletes, and entrepreneurs failing massively only to persevere through the next challenge, rising to success and fame. "Failure" is just another word for "learning opportunity." When we approach difficult situations as opportunities to learn, grow, and find success, we not only expand our potential for happiness, but our ability to see past life's challenges.

To embrace one's own struggles and failure, it helps to familiarize oneself with the stories of those whose journeys through trial and tribulation are powerful enough to inspire us. I, for instance, have always been motivated by the example of my own father. As I mentioned, he lost his own father before he was born, and as a teenager, he lost his left arm in a factory accident. Nevertheless, he persevered and worked hard his entire life. Ultimately, he became a successful businessman by building his own furniture company while raising nine children of his own and sponsoring hundreds of needy children. My father would start his day at 4:00 AM and work nonstop well into the evening. Regardless, he never allowed his rigorous schedule to interfere with his responsibilities as a son, husband, and father. I distinctly remember seeing him driving his truck with his one hand from city to city diligently handling his business affairs, and still leaving enough time to tend to his household duties. My mother did not drive or work outside the house, so my father's responsibilities, beyond managing his business, included all the external household work such as shopping and running errands around town, as well as driving my siblings and me to and from school every day. Throughout this flurry of constant and labor-intensive activity, I never heard him complain about his physical handicap, or use it as an excuse for why he could not accomplish something. If anything, he was proud of his self-sufficiency and ability to provide for his family and the many other families his factory employed.

When I reflect on the immense burdens he carried and the great joy and love with which he managed his responsibilities, my heart is rededicated to overcoming any relatively small adversity in my own life. This is not to dismiss the agony of one's unique experiences as we struggle through life's challenges. Sometimes challenges in life are exceptionally severe, making us feel as though they are insurmountable. Embracing that severity, however, is the first step to adopting the mindset that adverse conditions are merely a stepping stone to success.

Maintain Selective Attention

When striving for success, we must commit to reaching our goal with determination. The other side of this coin is "focus." All unhelpful stimuli should be removed from our lives so they do not distract us from our mission and purpose on earth. We need to have commitment, discipline, and consistency in our thoughts, actions, and lifestyles. We should be mindful of our physical and mental diets. In addition to making sure that what we eat and drink is natural and beneficial to our physical being, we must ensure that what we feed our mind is high quality as well. Just as any nutritionist or physician reminds us to avoid feeding our body junk food, sugary sodas, and other empty calories, we should aim to avoid toxic thoughts that poison our emotional systems and cripple our ability to function on a high spiritual level. Unfortunately, just as junk food has its own allure, we are naturally attracted to "bad news" or messages that stoke our anger, mistrust, and fear. News streams are rife with petty stories that mindlessly capture our attention. Our egos, subconsciously waiting for confirmation, are easily distracted by superficial digital socializing. We need to be conscious of what these messages do to our mental-emotional state, avoid taking in negative nutrition, and seek out ways to share positive messages to help keep others on a straight path as well.

To stay on the fast track to success and happiness, we must pay attention to only that which adds value to our lives and increases our capacity to learn and grow to our full potential. This means we must rid ourselves of inherited beliefs that unconsciously drain our ability to evolve both mentally and physically. When we make life choices without considering their purpose, we risk accidentally clinging to routines or habits passed down through our respective cultures without regard for their value within our own personal context. We must think critically in order to examine our assumptions about the world around us, as this will enable us to filter what does and does not deserve our attention. In doing so, we can focus our attention on information beneficial to us and our society, channel it into appropriate action, and raise collective consciousness.

Learn and Act Upon Knowledge

Everything we do starts with an idea. When we hold an idea in our mind, we hold the seed to a potential new reality. When contemplation of an idea or a plan leads to a joyful moment in the mind, we must then translate our ideas into action so we can benefit from the real experience. Positive feelings and thoughts have the potential to manifest into positive outcomes in reality. It is up to the individual to choose whether or not to work towards these goals. If we do not apply our mental vision to our physical reality, then the positive vibes and desired accomplishments will not materialize. When we do act upon our knowledge, however, we are able to align our visions for success with our lived experiences.

When one lacks enough information to make a decision in any scenario, one must also assume the responsibility for acquiring the knowledge requisite to make a fully informed decision. Choose not to research further runs the risk of squandering time and enabling failure by relying on standardized programs and systems that do not account for individual circumstances. Standardization is by definition not optimized to guarantee individual success, meaning a typical approach may not be best for a given situation. Regrettably, this was the case with my own family, and I hope this story will encourage others to first learn, then act.

The issue concerns the education of our children, who ranged in age from infant to teenager when our family relocated from New York to Arizona. Within a few years, our family gained first-hand experience with the whole spectrum of schooling options: public schools, charter schools, private schools including Montessori-inspired schools, and weekend religious schools. The diversity is not only due to our moving across the country: my husband and I had both attended school in similar, stable, private communities, and we were not familiar with the many other options. We were just trying to find the best learning environment for our kids.

But this lack of knowledge had an unexpected negative consequence, especially for our oldest son. He later joked with us that he felt like a guinea pig when recalling his adolescence shaped by experimental school-hopping, but it is a small miracle he can recall these times with good humor. As we changed up his learning environment, trying to find a good middle ground between his small, Algerian school and the massive institutions of metropolitan Phoenix, my eldest son felt trapped by being forced to learn the same material repetitively because he was not achieving the level of mastery as defined by the inflexible, standardized curriculum. He quickly became frustrated and bored, which further diminished his confidence and interest in school.

Teachers and administrators eventually labeled both of my older boys "learning disabled" and "ADHD."

It turned out that the administrator's intentions were in the right place, but the labels were not appropriate. However, when we initially heard their assessments, we felt scared of missing an opportunity to help our children, and bought into the labels and their implications. Even though on one level we did understand the nature of our sons' extenuating circumstances, specifically their unique cultural and linguistic background, we hesitated to pursue other options at this point out of concern for our kids' progress. Looking back, it is easy to regret not leaning into our understanding and pursuing more knowledge of different learning styles that could have accounted for our sons' atypical needs. Unfortunately, we blindly "followed the rules," and went the route of seeking advice from counselors, psychiatrists, and psychologists.

Thankfully, our delusion did not last long. Even as the boys underwent their battery of mental tests and analyses, I conducted my own research about child psychology and education. I studied the pharmaceutical industry, the overdiagnosis of ADHD, and the often questionable relationship between medical doctors and pharmaceutical companies. From our own experiences, we pieced the puzzle together and started to realize that our sons had been misdiagnosed and that their so-called "medications" were not the right answer. We looked to alternative teaching and learning methods and pursued tutoring when necessary. However, my oldest son was at this point a young adult, and had given up on the formal education system, choosing instead to pursue his own path to learning and success.

In sharing my family's experience, I hope to express the importance of the individual valuing one's own life and learning experiences. Do not let fear get in the way of gaining knowledge through experience. What a person learns from experience is the best, most tangible form of knowledge, even if it deviates from the norm. You learn best by engaging with life on all levels, not just by internalizing the static lessons taught in books or lectures. Knowledge gained through experience is probably the best source of information and understanding you can apply to direct your own personal life journey forward. Make choices that leverage your knowledge and stimulate your passion in order to help to fully motivate yourself to take the final steps toward action or implementation. Then, when you are confident in your knowledge gained through study and experience, the time has come to act. Only when we complete this process of learning, experiencing, and implementation are we capable of ultimately benefiting from what we have learned. Knowledge and experience without action is ripe fruit left on the vine to wither and die.

Of course, many situations call for us to learn and implement our knowledge gradually. A poorly considered action plan may actually result in a worse outcome plagued with despair and regret. How many people attempt to instantiate a new diet or habit, and rush into three days of frenetic activity only to abandon the project entirely within a week's time? At times it may be better to make life changes one step at a time, to become accustomed to new habits and build consistency with a measured approach over a planned period of time. Without consistent actions, our lives will be full of either dreams of what we want to do, or regrets for what we have not done. These feelings of longing remove our concentration and focus from the present moment. When we adjust our actions one step at a time, our focus remains present and our minds stay clear, so, as we approach our goals, we become better able to receive information and guidance from the higher consciousness. As we act on this new knowledge that is built upon a solid foundation of good habits, we start to build confidence in ourselves, further affirming that the power of change originates inside of us.

In my experience, I have learned that the most important step when heading down the path of knowledge is to focus on what we want, the point of origin of all action. If we are creators of our own reality, we need to focus on learning what is right for us and our own situations, and commit to act upon this knowledge in order to realize the best-possible potential fruit. Only once we align our aspirations to both our physical reality and higher levels of consciousness are we able to achieve the ultimate measure of success.

Forgive

Forgiveness is the process of removing sin, guilt, and regret from the self. It is a natural part of life to experience traumas and disappointments such as the loss of a job or even the death of a loved one. These are challenges we expect to have, as they are embedded in the human experience. The best way to respond to such difficulties is not to lament but rather, after grieving, to brush yourself off, forgive yourself and others, rest, and learn from your losses.

After experiencing loss, many people remain stuck in thought cycles of anger and despair. Emotions begin to rule their lives and their actions, and they continue to suffer. They may attempt to get over the emotional pain with superficial methods like painkillers and medicine, but these do not truly heal the suffering. It is actually the spiritual self, not the physical self, that needs acknowledgment and balm, for release from suffering.

Forgiveness comes in several forms. The self

needs forgiveness for unwittingly extending suffering and succumbing to negative emotions. One needs to apply forgiveness to one's difficult situation and the other actors in it, so one is not burdened by anger or regret. If we over-focus on the difficult emotions that cause discomfort and imbalance, we may become disconnected from our goals and objectives, perhaps permanently. However, if we forgive ourselves and others, we are able to overcome obstacles and move on, progressing towards our purpose in life. Hard knocks teach us how to better handle trauma, and help us gain compassion for others experiencing difficult times. Practicing forgiveness, for ourselves and others, enables us to find gratitude even when faced with difficult learning experiences.

Banish Fear With Hope

Our bodies have developed myriad response mechanisms to anticipate, interpret, and respond to perceived dangers. One of our most basic instincts is fear, and its purpose is to initiate the "fight or flight" response mechanism, an important survival tool. However, fear can also cause anxiety, leading to depression and other mental illnesses. It is crucial for us to moderate our response to fear, as not all situations are life-threatening. Our purpose as spiritual beings is to eliminate our fears and to grow instead a sense of optimism and hope. Instead of focusing on the fear of the unknown, we need to replace it with hope for prosperity and strength. As we are blessed with free will, instead of allowing fear and negativity to dominate our mind, we can and should train our mind to focus on thoughts of wealth, peace, and comfort.

Sincere hope can propel us towards unexpected success. When I arrived in Syracuse from Algeria for the second time, I began searching for a scholarship, any scholarship, in any department, at SU. I fueled my mission with pure hope that a door would open, that some opportunity would arise. Upon arrival, I did not know a single soul on campus. I had no connections and no advisors to help guide me along. The admissions department informed me that I was required to take the Graduate Records

Examination (GRE) to qualify for any type of scholarship. So, I prepared for the exam, studying hard so I could pass. In the meantime, I happened to meet a professor in the Mechanical Engineering department. Fortuitously, we discussed my curriculum vitae from Constantine University and my love of mathematics and physics. He showed me some of his research in the mechanics of materials (elasticity and plasticity), and gave me some books and a few mathematical "problems" to evaluate. In our second meeting, I demonstrated my comprehension of the material and my ability to work through the derivations of the formulas and solutions. Upon seeing this, the professor was so impressed that he offered me a spot in the PhD program with a Teaching Assistantship, and to my great delight, he also waived the need for me to take the GRE. Soon thereafter, he became my academic advisor, and in a few months I began instructing sophomores in Engineering Statics by helping them with homework during recitation periods. The situation was even better than I had hoped for!

Accept Alternatives

Sometimes, even when we adopt a mindset of gratitude, equip ourselves with knowledge, and approach all obstacles with forgiveness and hope, we are still not rewarded with our expected result. This is not an indication of failure, however. You need to have confidence and comfort yourself that any ultimate result is what is best for you at that time, even if it exhibits apparent setbacks or deviations from your original plan.

My career path provides my handiest example. In my early academic life, when I was studying at university, I never imagined myself starting my own school. My professional energy was focused on becoming a university professor. I was concurrently raising a young and expanding family, though, and domestic life-related obstacles never ceased. Many personal ambitions were frequently put on hold so I could address the needs of my family, from birthing my children to supervising the education and social lives of the six kids through our two cross-country moves over a period of six years. Thankfully, I did not lament that my career path was winding around my family, or I might have missed an important opportunity: my intense focus on my own children's education planted the seeds that ultimately resulted in the opening of my own learning center.

Love Others As You Love Yourself

"You will not attain faith in God until you have love for others as you have love for yourself." ~Muhammad

This saying attributed to the Prophet Muhammad teaches us that love will help establish a peaceful community. My mother always taught me that the best way to test the extent of our consciousness is by expressing unconditional love to others. After all, a person cannot truly love other people until he chooses to understand others as passionately and deeply as he understands himself. To wit, the quality of the love that people direct towards others is a reflection of that person's inner state of being. When we express a love-energy toward others that is commensurate to the love we take for ourselves, we are able to empower other people by enabling them to be the best version of themselves.

One way of expressing love for other people is by choosing to live a life that allows us to contribute positively to others' well-being. We are most likely to act on this mission with enthusiasm when we concurrently pursue our passions. One's generosity toward others may be reflected in the type of career one chooses, such as teaching or counseling, or it may manifest itself in personal habits, such as acting with empathy. I remember my mother used to grow herbs such as mint, cilantro, and parsley. When at the market among the homeless people, she would invite them to freely pick herbs from her garden so that they could make some money selling them. Later on, back at the market, she would buy her herbs back from them. My mother was constantly thinking of others, trying to find clever, new ways to create jobs for those who needed them and alleviate their hardship.

Loving generously is not always easy. Too easily we can become attached to our own selves, our own shells, our own stuff. Of these three, it is the last category that is the easiest to sacrifice. Thus, I believe that the easiest way to enable a mindset of giving freely is to detach ourselves from material possessions, and to always remain conscious of our mortality. As we depart this world, we are forever divorced from all material possessions. This certainly does not mean we should not engage in life, to work hard for and enjoy the things we own. It is just that an awareness of our physical impermanence should prevent us from becoming overly attached to material things.. As Ali ibn Abi Talib stated, "Detachment is not that you do not own anything, but that the things you own should not own you." In many ways, death is a great teacher and we should take a moment to remember it daily as it is our doorway to true, fully-realized life. At the very least, it can remind us to be generous and loving with other people.

Open Your Mind To New Consciousness

Since a very young age I have woken up daily

around 4:00 am. I pray *fajr* (the morning prayer in Islam) and sit to ponder the universe. As a married woman with six children, the early morning was the only time I could read, study, and pray by myself before the daily life of a mother began. At some point, I noticed that my morning routine, which included sitting in reflection both before and after prayer, brought me waves of awareness, insight, and positive feelings. It is critical to realize that knowledge is not gained solely through physical senses and formal cognitive education. We can also "download" a higher knowledge from sources of consciousness beyond our easily accessible physical reality. Our dreams, meditations, reflections, and solitary moments can all serve as modalities of connection to higher forms of knowledge.

Here is an old story of mine about gaining knowledge through dreams. When I was fourteen years old, my family was preparing for my oldest sister's engagement party. My mother was busy shopping for a fifty-person party and she explained to me that there would be much work to do. That very night, in my dreams, I saw that only three people were going to attend the party, not the fifty that mother was expecting. Furthermore, there was to be someone else in attendance, a man with a beard, someone whom I did not recognize. Instead of stressing over party preparations, I felt relaxed, knowing that the work we were doing was more than enough for the actual number of guests I expected to attend. In the end, only three people attended due to an emergency in the groom's family. Afterwards, my mom's bearded cousin showed up, a man whom I had not seen in many years. Even though the ramifications of this particular foresight were not particularly profound or impactful in a greater sense, it left an indelible mark in my mind about the gravity and importance of being aware of intuitions and insights that arrive in the mind almost serendipitously. Expanding our awareness and being open to a greater range of information that is floating through our apparent reality is important for developing an intuitive sense of the world around us.

I experienced another significant dream as an adult. In spring 2001, before waking to pray and meditate, I dreamt of my Uncle Issa who had been deceased for ten years. He told me that I would have a boy and that he (Issa) would take my father away before my child would be born. Pregnant at the time, I was indeed anticipating the visit of my father, a man who, by any measure, appeared quite healthy. Later in the morning, when I was driving to my teaching job, all I could think about was my dream and the potential significance of the message I received from my deceased uncle. Later on, I told my mother and siblings about my unusual dream. Of course it was difficult for everyone to believe that such a strange and foreboding dream could possibly be true, until a few months later when my father was suddenly diagnosed with liver cancer. He passed away later that summer, just two weeks before my son was born. Looking back, I try to imagine the shock I would have felt if his diagnosis had come as a surprise, especially during pregnancy! How would I have handled the situation, and how would it have affected me in such a vulnerable state? Instead, by being open, and tuned-in to the possibility of receiving information from beyond the realm of conscious experience, I was able to mentally and emotionally prepare for an otherwise unknown, unexpected, and difficult reality. Ultimately, I felt lucky to have had the opportunity to prepare myself for this calamitous event, especially considering my sensitive state at the time.

Higher levels of knowledge cannot be accessed only through dreams or meditations. These insights can also arrive from feelings of intuition, or "gut feelings." It can be difficult to acknowledge these internal whisperings, especially when they suggest less popular courses of action. After all, it is often easier to cruise on auto-pilot, assuming those attributed particular authority such as medical doctors and traditional religious authorities offer superior guidance. While following one's own inner compass may seem to shake the foundation of our reality, ignoring its promptings prevents us from awakening our own innate ability to intuit the fabric of our own lives as it is being woven around us.

For many years I fought a chronic illness, lupus. I spent much time and energy researching the disease and consulting with various doctors and specialists. I tried multiple medicines and treatments, including experimental chemotherapy.

As my condition worsened, my husband ended up taking me to the emergency room several times a year. It became clear that the remedies provided by the doctors of conventional medicine, and, more broadly, the allopathic medical system, were not helping me. My perpetual illness led the experts to determine that my disease was incurable. When I started seeking a solution to my condition by using natural methods of healing, I encountered energy healing through meditation. I realized that my illnesses were the result of a combination of stress, negative energy, and poor diet. I had to cure myself through my own actions, my own lifestyle adjustments. There was no magic pill, no specialist in a white coat that could deliver a technological wonder to resolve my issues. I overcame the disease, and many of the physical ailments resolved, to the extent that my primary care physician declared me to be in remission. The huge success of following my intuition and leaning on my meditation practice reinforced my belief that information and truth is not only found in the established, authoritative systems.

Meditation is well-established in both the

medical profession and so many traditions around the world, including Islam. In addition to the rich Sufi traditions, the Qur'an prescribes meditation as a wonderful method for achieving spiritual success. Qur'anic verse 16:79 (Surah al-Isra') reads,"Be still during some of the night; it is an addition to your life, and maybe your Lord will send you to a blessed spiritual station." This verse contains the only instance of the etymological root "*h-j-d*" in the Qur'an. The uniqueness of this word's appearance associates it with the uniqueness of God, drawing our attention to its meaning. When we investigate the meaning of this root in classical dictionaries, such as *Maqayīs al-Lugha*, we find that its core meaning is "stillness, keeping oneself still." Also, in Surah al-Sharh, meditation is mentioned as a method to "expand our chest" to be able to receive information from the divine source. These are the only verses in the entire Qur'an that I have understood to indicate meditation in the most commonly understood sense of the word. I find these occurrences interesting considering most people do not think of "Eastern-style" meditation as having any relevance within traditionally practiced Islam.

Difference Between Meditation and Ritual Prayer

Meditation (traditional, "Eastern-style" meditation) is vastly different from ritual prayer. Meditation's primary focus is the current moment of opportunity to take something in (subconscious realizations, cosmic wisdom, etc.). In meditation we turn towards the spiritual self and away from the finite, reductionist mind to sink into the infinite awareness of God within us, allowing us to lull in peace. The stillness is like being asleep while still awake, and when we come out of a deep meditation we find ourselves waking up to reality. Incorporating daily meditation into our self-care regimen allows us to live more securely in our natural state of awareness of true existence. What a practical and comparably more beneficial alternative to the temporary joys people often seek in the external world!

In contrast to the inward turning of

meditation, ritual prayer, while also peaceful, regular, and involving movement and recitation, intends to send messages outward (expressions of gratitude and worship and hope). In Islam, we stand up, bend, prostrate, and recite the Qur'an and other prayers, expressing thankfulness. During the prayer process, Muslims experience a special type of mental stillness, however the process is primarily centered on remembering God and verbally and internally expressing gratitude for gifts granted.

Developing practices of meditation and prayer gives us a sense of permanent joy and the power to face any obstacle. By incorporating positive affirmations into our meditative practice, we are able to both support and reinforce our beliefs and actively work toward accomplishing our desired goals. Perhaps more specifically, meditation on gratitude, love, forgiveness, patience, and excellence is key to keeping our minds and hearts on track.

3

GATEKEEPERS VS. DOOR OPENERS

The spiritual strength-training of meditation prepares us to combat the restrictive attitudes of the "gatekeepers" we encounter throughout our lives, those people, institutions or ideas that aim to prevent us from reaching toward the higher consciousness, to prevent us from achieving our goals. Those entities who facilitate smooth passage as we progress towards spiritual fulfilment, alternatively, are like "door openers," those who exist to aid and direct us on our journeys. I reflect on my own personal experiences relative to "gatekeepers" and "door openers".

As a young child I always enjoyed playing stone games like jacks and checkers with my friends and cousins in our backyard. To their dismay, I always won because I could quickly count and perform the mental calculations necessary to predict the optimal next move. One day my uncle, who had been observing us play, commented to me, "You have a talent, the most powerful kind to have. Go ahead and use it before you lose it." Of course at the time I did not understand the implications of his advice. Later, after learning mathematical concepts and how to apply them to a variety of subjects, I came to understand that my uncle was what one such "door opener." My love of mathematics grew with time and eventually I developed strong critical thinking skills, especially once exposed to algebra in the fifth grade.

Later in my adult life when I became a college math instructor, I learned that many students experience fear and anxiety about learning math. When I inquired and dug further into the matter, I found that the students' apprehension was often the result of a previous teacher or other mentor that had inadvertently contributed to their angst or dislike of learning math. People, methods, or institutions that block our progress are like guardians at the gate of knowledge and learning.

In many ways the student or young learner becomes intimidated by a subject or feels they are not worthy, not talented enough, or not possessing the aptitude to learn. Such "gatekeepers" are not consciously aware of or intentionally trying to discourage others from learning, in fact, it may be that they are simply not capable of instilling the confidence and desire required to explore challenging subjects.

Amid all the troubles I was facing during my first marriage, I was blessed to meet people from all over the world in those difficult years. One of the most influential people in my life was my good friend and neighbor Evelyn, a woman 60 years my elder. Although our friendship lasted a mere two years prior to her passing, Evelyn served as a great support in my life and advised me to push hard in my journey of learning. She helped me explore places in the U.S. and to learn English, which opened up so many doors for me, enabling me to read American texts. Even though she grew up Catholic and I was Muslim, we were highly connected as humans and never judged one other based on our religious backgrounds. I consider Evelyn to be a door opener in my life as she introduced me to the world and people outside of my own culture and belief system. It was through Evelyn that I learned that though we have different beliefs, we are all equal as humans and we can coexist together. Her final piece of advice to me before she passed away was that I should remain open to learning about life and consciousness, and that all humans come from the same Source. Evelyn's advice combined with my knowledge that powerful people have used religion throughout history to sow division, helped me maintain my focus on the universal truths that surround and govern us all. There is no reason to dwell on the superficial differences between people when, in reality, we are all from the same Source. My exposure to Evelyn's wisdom and the intellectual resonances we shared about fundamental aspects of life were an invaluable experience that helped to shape me as a young adult.

Some of the door openers who have impacted me are, in fact, individuals I have never met. Many scholars throughout history have been recognized as door openers for humanity, people who made historical contributions to intellectual advancement. For example, al-Khawarizmi, the mathematician known for introducing algebra (*al-jabr*) to Europe, wrote extensively on not only math, but also metaphysics, specifically, the relationship between mind, body, and spirit and the origins of consciousness. He is a role model and inspiration to me, and his achievements and philosophy motivated me to establish a new curriculum, something unique that differentiates NLC from other, traditional Sunday schools. Even though our lives are separated by more than a thousand years, he is still a door opener in my life because his contribution to the universe encouraged me to apply my capabilities and ideas in a new, unorthodox manner.

We should consider ourselves lucky when we meet a real door opener in the flesh. It is no wonder that our encounters with door openers are few and far between. I always wanted to be a door opener to my students whether in college where I taught math, or in my private institution, NLC. Our modern society highly values both conformity and mundane, product-oriented task completion at whatever mental cost. This effectively stymies educators who may otherwise challenge orthodoxy and set students upon a path of true exploration. From early on, children educated in the public school system are disconnected from the actual purpose of education; to expand the mind's powers. We see this disconnect in every aspect of the curriculum, and mathematics is no exception. Most present-day institutions teach "math facts" that are nothing more than a toolset for problem solving, and, unfortunately, educators do not allow students the opportunity to apply these tools in either a practical or creative manner. Rather, the latest teaching methods focus simply on showing students methodologies to solve problems without allowing them to persevere through the struggle of learning, to develop their own hardened approach to problem-solving. In reality, the greatest benefit of studying mathematics is that it helps to develop a student's logical and critical thinking abilities. A student properly trained in mathematics will learn how to work through and solve not just geometry and calculus, but real life problems as well.

My own children suffered from a prominent example of gatekeeping in our society, namely, the liberal diagnosis of and subsequent pharmaceutical intervention to "alleviate" symptoms of "atypical" behavior. America has a well-documented and exceptionally large percentage of children diagnosed with psychological conditions, specifically ADD and ADHD. Children diagnosed as such might not act neurotypical from the DSM's (Diagnostic and Statistical Manual of Mental Disorders) perspective, but their unique natures should not automatically be considered problematic. Many children with these "diagnoses" are incredibly gifted, fast and creative thinkers, and capable of multitasking very productively. Yet, instead of teaching these children strategies to harness their mental powers, parents, doctors, and schoolteachers often advocate for medication to quiet the electrical storms in the childrens' brains.

To my dismay, the adults most prominently positioned to open doors for such children may regrettably end up closing them instead. Research shows that adults who were medicated for these "disorders" as children display a greater tendency towards bipolar disorder, depression, and other challenges later in life. As a parent of a son who was diagnosed and medicated beginning in middle school, I can attest to the enormous emotional difficulty he continues to experience when he takes mind-altering medication. What if students like my son were allowed to live in their natural, unmedicated state? What if they were encouraged to accept themselves the way they were born, guided by mentors or door openers to leverage their innate abilities instead of humbly accept the "problematic" brand? Who knows the bounds of what they could accomplish and how they could thrive if provided with an environment conducive to their unique characteristics, instead of being silenced with pharmaceuticals. Attempting to close stifle the mind of a young person is one of the worst forms of gatekeeping there is. Children are natural learners, and are born with an instinct for creative, critical thinking. Curiosity and the capacity for logic is inherent to our *fiṭra* (intuition), our natural mental state. Attempting to dim their natal spark is tantamount to a rejection of their capacity to channel the higher consciousness in uniquely productive ways.

It is not only people and institutions that can stand as gatekeepers to human progress. Ideas can also serve in the same capacity. With respect to the Qur'an, there are numerous examples in the present day where peoples' misconceptions about specific language used in the Qur'an have lead them to believe that Islam is a violent and misogynistic religion. Unfortunately, these misunderstandings and poor interpretations block people from taking a closer look at Islam due to preconceived notions that the Qur'an offers nothing but negativity. Nothing could be further from the truth, but it takes a tremendous amount of interpretive work, understanding of historical context, and knowledge about the political power structures that have contributed to the control of Qur'anic messaging over the past 1,500 years to overcome such a strong social stigma and accepted misinterpretation. Understanding the Qur'an is not a simple task of just picking up a translation, reading an interpretation suited for your native tongue, and arriving at a lucid understanding of the original Arabic text. Much work has to be done to bring the Qur'an into a contextualized and accurately translated form that is capable of adequately delivering the intended message from Muhammad's time.

For example, one of the common misconceptions is that the Qur'an not only condones but encourages the beating of wives as an acceptable method of punishment by husbands. This false idea, due to a poor interpretation and translation of verse 4:34 (al-Nisa'), perpetuates the negative aura surrounding the Qur'an in the minds of many. This misunderstanding of the Qur'an's message directly contradicts the numerous calls for equal treatment of men and women and the establishment of universal justice, two concepts delivered in very strong terms throughout the text. From a logical perspective, it simply does not make sense for God to continually express the importance of justice being served on Earth whilst simultaneously calling for the physical abuse of 50% of the people inhabiting the planet. How is it possible that physical abuse of loved ones can coincide in a text that repeatedly calls for fairness, justice, and equality? It is possible that some interpretations (born from western society) of Qur'anic text may have been influenced by patriarchal tendencies. It is not too far-fetched to assume that willful misinterpretations and ulterior motives have contributed to the contradiction in messaging, skewing peoples' understanding of Islamic values.

From a historical perspective, one of the most widely known examples of attempted, and thwarted, gate-keeping is the story of the prophet Abraham and the disagreement he had with his father about the idols or man-made objects of worship. In this tale, common to all three major monotheistic world religions, Abraham courageously stands up to his father, smashing the idols worshipped by the people at that time. His objective was to emphasize the unique and indivisible nature of God, a reality Abraham discovered through meditative exploration. The immense courage Abraham required to take such bold, heretical action against idols perceived by many to be actual gods provides a succinct message for everyone of faith: to realize the best versions of ourselves, we must defy those who attempt to repress the energies inside of us that strive to align with the Higher Consciousness. If logic and reason provide clear evidence that status quo behavior does not stand up to critique, then one must follow one's heart and mind to ensure that truth is revealed to those suppressed under gimmick and falsehood.

As previously mentioned, one of the objectives throughout my career as a teacher, both in a collegiate setting and at NLC, has been to find ways to inspire students to rise above their own personal challenges and become the best possible versions of themselves. I believe that a teacher has an obligation to not only provide a challenging educational experience, but to deliver information in a compassionate manner, realizing that all individuals exist on different planes with different interests, capabilities, and life experiences. Being sensitive to these diversities whilst impressing upon students a challenging, often unorthodox, education is the essence of what I aim to accomplish. This desire to challenge and inspire students burns inside me, and offers me, too, the motivation to become the best possible version of myself. One of my long-standing hopes is to become a door-opener for others so that I may pass along the benefits given to me from the door openers who helped me in my life journey. A few students from NLC were gracious enough to share their stories and experiences on how NLC classes impacted their lives.

The following personal stories are shared here not as an effort to "evangelize" or for this author's self promotion, but to serve as examples of how an opened door allows students to gain insight and make spiritual progress. It just happens that the context involves developing a clearer understanding of the Qur'an and Islam. In these cases, the opened door enabled these people to find truth using the tools of language and their intellect to get past cultural baggage that the gate-keepers of conventional thought have upheld for centuries by prioritizing rules, social regulations, and ritual practices over critical examination of source material. Here are their stories:

Nasri's Journey:
Connecting to Islam for the First Time

Although born into Islam, I was never really interested in organized religion due to its association with a history of control, wars, and violence. I, like many others, considered myself a seeker of truth and justice. After the tragic events of 9/11 and my subsequent joining of the 9/11 truth movements, I was forced to take a deeper look into my birth religion at that time. Feeling that Islam was the closest thing to truth, I embraced it and embarked on a journey, spending the next ten years researching and learning more about religious ideologies, their evolutions, and the dogma that encloses them. I stopped becoming a truth-seeker and transitioned more into a door-opener for Islam. I was teaching youth, visiting prisons, and helping to spread the message of Islam, even though I knew that the mainstream implementation of Islam fell short of its actual ideals.

My reason for joining NLC as an instructor in 2011 was to continue my efforts as a door-opener for people interested in Islam. It was at NLC where certain questions and information began to emerge, challenging my understanding and leading to further investigations. Specifically, there were questions in my mind about the pivotal moment after the death of Prophet Mohammad. In Sunni Islam, the community of people that lived amongst the prophet are considered to be infallible, however, at the same time, these same people are viewed as criminals from the Shi'a perspective. This tension was too important for me to overlook as I had realized a similar theme when studying the history of Christianity, notably the role of Paul and Constantine in the development of institutionalized Christianity. After that epiphany, I transitioned back into a truth-seeker, eager and willing to remove all historical filters to take a fresh look at Islam.

With Fatima's help, I learned to read the Qur'an in a literal and liberating way. It is the way that Islam had always been approached since Islam's infancy, however, as history shows time and time again, powerful forces have a tendency to control the narratives. That being said, there have been great scholars, such as Muhammad Abduh, who started a period of Islamic enlightenment by taking a rational and linguistic approach to the Qur'an. It is said that many Islamic sects today reference Muhammad Abduh as their leader, however none implement his methodology. More recently, intellectuals such as

Muhammad Shahrur have had a positive impact by revealing some of the distortions that have been imposed upon the Qur'an over the years. Adding to this body of historical dissent, the work done at NLC has helped to advance the effort of truth in a reasonable, logical manner. I am fortunate to have found a place in my backyard that applies Abduh's methodology in search of Islamic truth.

The linguistic approach to the Qur'an that NLC follows, helps to establish a wider and more substantial message that centers on the concept of justice for the widest possible audience-- literally, the world community. The NLC approach embraces both scientific and historically controversial topics such as creation vs evolution, "sticky" religious topics such as jinns and polygamy, and the discretely social topics such as adoption in Islam. The range of exploration is as limitless as the human experience. I applaud Fatima's efforts through NLC to allow the Qur'an to speak for itself by applying a methodology that is foundational to the history of Islam.

Authoug's Story:
A Journey to an Expanded Understanding of Islam

I met Fatima El-Hindi in my late twenties. I was born a Muslim and followed the traditions taught to me in childhood. My faith in God was strong and I thought that I understood Islam. I looked at the Qur'an as a book with loving, healing words, a book that was a constant reminder that God would always protect us. I did not realize that the Qur'an was so much more.

At the time I met Fatima, my life had shifted into unknown territory. I was newly divorced and raising two children. The future was unclear, but I knew that God would protect me and I needed to complete my education. Education is extremely important to my parents and they believed it was the only way for me to build a strong future. I felt that these were two different entities, faith and education. I did not realize that I was very wrong. To become a true Muslim, I needed to be educated, and, to be educated, I needed to truly understand the Qur'an. To grow and learn on

Earth we need both, the spiritual and the academic.

Fatima taught that the Qur'an was based on science and that it is a universal guide for all mankind. Through her classes, she explained how the Qur'an should be used as a tool to uncover the meaning of life and beyond. She dissected vocabulary from the Qur'an, researching the original meaning from the time of the prophets. I realized that although the Qur'an has never been changed, the true meaning had been altered and hidden. An individual word could have multiple meanings based on what the "scholars" wanted adherents to believe and understand for a specific verse.

Fatima had her students question their own traditions and practices. I slowly began to realize I did not know the Qur'an at all. The traditions that I had followed were nowhere to be found in the Qur'an. In childhood, I was listening and learning about stories that were told to each generation by our elders. The science and facts in the Qur'an had been lost and were not passed down.

I always enjoyed the stories of the past and accepted the teachings of the elders. We were taught not to ask too many questions and accept that some questions were to stay unanswered. I had also been busy with the material world and many family and community obligations, so I did not put too much thought into analyzing the Qur'an in my own time. I believed the Qur'an simply told stories of the past and protected us from evil.

Fatima slowly reintroduced us to the Qur'an. She exposed us to the expanded vocabulary, had us ask questions and showed us how different ideas were connected in the Qur'an. I slowly began to see the Qur'an in a new light in which justice, love of humanity and equality prevailed. It was not just filled with fairy tales, but historical facts that people can learn and grow from. It describes historical figures that showed exceptional character and morals. It highlights people that have made mistakes and learned from them, and yet others that have failed their test on Earth. I relearned the Qur'an, and was exposed to the very practical answers to real world problems that are described within.

I began to look at the Qur'an as a manual to life. My education in school and my life experiences were fitting together so perfectly with the body of knowledge in the Qur'an. I realized how short our life on Earth is, and just how much there is to understand. I began to look at how amazing everything around me really was, from the plants I grew in my backyard to the sun setting in the evening. I also became more aware of the many injustices in the world. I felt more responsible for the pain people were going through even if it was experienced on the other side of the world. I realized the interconnectedness of humanity, and how important it is to have empathy for each other.

Fatima continuously emphasized the importance of community and that all humanity is connected. "We are one microfiber from the same cloth," Fatima said to me one day. Empathy is an important emotion to continue to build within myself. Without empathy you can never really feel the pain of others, which means you cannot understand them. If you can not understand a neighbor, friend, or co-worker, how can you be a good neighbor, friend, or co-worker? If I am unable to empathize with the parent of one of my students, I can never teach them as if they were my own child. I would teach the child as if they were a stranger, the student would feel that disconnect, and she would not learn. Simultaneously, I would be wasting my time teaching them. Empathy has made me kinder, more aware and more sensitive to the world around me. I began to sympathize with people because I felt sorry that they did not understand the bigger picture. As I grew spiritually, the sympathy grew into empathy, a more complex emotion, enabling me to actually experience their pain. Anger and hatred can not enter your heart when you feel the pain of another person.

Fatima showed me that there is so much more to the Qur'an than what I was taught. Answers to questions about myself, the world and beyond. There is so much I do not know but every tiny bit of information that is uncovered fills my heart with more love for the Qur'an. Although I am learning new ideas and information, the integration of new information has always felt right, nothing has ever gone against my soul, beliefs, or energy. All the information has come together like a puzzle. I have applied what I have learned to heal myself and to live a better life.

Through Fatima's teaching, I discovered that the Qur'an is a guide for life, a guide for how to be successful on Earth. The Qur'an provides details about the challenges we must overcome and how to address them. The universal laws of human nature are explained. The importance of positivity, generosity, honesty, and community are repeated throughout the Qur'an. Lives of righteous people are described as well as the hardships they faced and the paths they took. The Qur'an explains our purpose for being here on Earth and provides a look at what is to come in the hereafter.

From my life's experience working and learning with Fatima, I consider her my door-opener to the true Islam. She showed me how much more there is to life and beyond. She revealed the importance of being grateful for every small gift given to us from something as simple as our fingers to something more complex like the material wealth we build over a lifetime. She helped me to realize that our imperfections are a gift from which to learn and grow even if the task is difficult and time-consuming. Every day is a new opportunity to become a better person and to unlock the mysteries of the universe. There is so much to understand and learn, and I am grateful for the journey ahead of me.

Daniel's Story:
Modernizing Islam is the Right "Fit" for a Multicultural Family

As a bi-racial, multicultural family we were having difficulty finding a suitable Sunday school program for our son. Our desire was to raise him with a knowledge of and appreciation for all religions and philosophies, but also make certain he gained a deeper exposure to Islam specifically. My wife, born and raised in Malaysia yet a citizen of the United States, was concerned our son would grow up a "typical" American kid, having no knowledge of or interest in his mother's native culture or her religious foundation.

For a short while our son attended Sunday school at a local mosque. Considering the relatively small number of Muslims in our area the options were limited, so we accepted what was available. Immediately, the sternly patriarchal vibe of the mosque revealed itself, putting us in the uncomfortable position of tolerating an environment that went against our beliefs in order to gain access to the Muslim community and some of the basic teachings. The environment at the mosque felt punitive, divisive straight away; men yelling at young boys playing and having fun, young boys and girls separated from one another, and a primary focus on the rote, ritualistic aspects of prayer and Qur'an recitation. After a year of enduring an environment that stood in opposition to our views of a tolerant, open-minded Islam, we learned about the Nas Learning Center run by Fatima El-Hindi.

It was immediately apparent that Fatima was focused on creating an unorthodox Islamic experience for the kids. Instead of a primary focus on parroting Qur'an verses in an unknown tongue as many non-Arabic speaking kids are required to do in Islamic school, actual learning is the center of the experience. Instead of wasting energy worrying about the "correct" time to stand, kneel, prostrate, and bow during prayers, NLC is focused on teaching kids the basics of Arabic grammar through allegory, real world situations, and of course surahs as well. In addition to grammar studies, the stories of the Qur'an are leveraged to teach the children not only about God and creation but about the responsibilities placed on members of a community, the importance of having respect for others, and how to be the best person possible in a diverse, inclusive world. The experience has been positive not only for my wife, who now feels a greater sense of religious and cultural anchoring in the community, but also for my son, who has made some good friends and greatly expanded his awareness of what Islam entails and what it means to "be a Muslim."

In addition to our son having access to a rich, expansive and modern Islamic education, my wife has also grown significantly from attending Fatima's lectures at NLC. Having spent her formative years learning the myths, legends, and cultural tales of traditional Islam, she was pleasantly shocked to have the blinders removed from her eyes. Fatima's linguistic analysis of the

Qur'an resulted in my wife questioning everything she thought she knew about the religion of her birth. Through a deeper analysis of root meaning, Fatima exposed my wife to the essence of Islam. By focusing solely on the message of the Qur'an and not muddying the waters with hearsay, superstition, unjustified tradition, or mindless, ritualistic mechanics, Fatima has helped to uncover the spiritual authenticity and richness of Islam. From deconstructing and reinterpreting well-known stories in the Qur'an to the healing powers of meditation, to a heated discussion on the true meaning of a word as loaded as "halal," Fatima has helped to open my wife's mind to the possibility that Islam, and specifically the contents of the Qur'an, are much broader, deeper and nuanced than the patriarchal powers over the last millennia would have one believe. It is always an interesting Sunday when my wife comes home after Sunday school and says, "You won't believe what I learned in Fatima's class today…" Our adventure in learning through Nas Learning Center has opened doors for me and my family to better understand Islam.

4

TESTS IN LIFE ARE UNIVERSAL

As I write this book amid the COVID-19 pandemic of 2020, I am strongly reminded of the fact that much of what happens in life occurs beyond our control. When times are worry-free it is easy to be complacent, living life as if we are the masters in control of our own little piece of Earth. However, when struggles arise, we are jolted out of our comfortable realities and forced to pick up the shattered pieces, to keep moving forward. Many people, the world over, have been ripped from their known lives and are struggling to deal with hardships and the unknown. Beyond the primary concern of health, people are dealing with lost jobs, food insecurity, separation, mental illness, and concerns of freedom, security and the open question of what the future will look like.

All of us have been presented with challenges, and how we focus our energies going forward will determine not only our survival but our success on the other side of this tragedy.

From my perspective, as COVID-19 started spreading and becoming a real threat, I began to calmly prepare my school for the possibility of having to shift to virtual learning. Myriad new issues and problems had to be resolved quickly. I was bombarded with messages from teachers and parents who expressed agitation and worry. Some parents, out of fear for an uncertain future, wanted to stop tuition payments or be released from their contracts, putting the financial future of the school in jeopardy. Even after establishing a basic methodology for online learning, video streaming tools presented numerous technical challenges, especially for the teachers with little to no experience with virtual instruction. Of course I found myself dealing with the typical issues of every school semester, however, this time around, the heightened emotional state of everyone involved made for an exceptionally chaotic scramble to ensure not only the school's continuance but its very survival.

Amid the chaos, I found it interesting that the teachers, parents, and community members within our school, though they come from all over the world, exhibited a similar response to this global stressor. These normal human behaviors are instilled in all of us, and when something triggers our fight-or-flight survival response, they emerge; the fear and concern of the unknown. However, even though these responses are woven into the fabric of our being, we still have the ability to control how these emotions affect our behaviors. One of our purposes here on Earth is to wrestle control of our emotions, to explicitly chart an individual path forward and to grow as a fragment of a greater consciousness. To gain a better understanding of the universality of our experiences, we need only look to our common origin as described in Qur'anic verses 76:1-3 (al-Insan):

1. Has there come upon humans a period of time when they were not remembered?
2. We created the human from a drop of

mixed fluid to test him; and thus we made him hearing and seeing.

3. Indeed, we guided him to the path, whether he is grateful or ungrateful.

Amazingly, these verses predate our modern scientific understanding of the "drop" of liquid that contains all of the genetic material required to develop a fully functioning human. The verses continue on, explaining the fact that humans are endowed with the ability to hear and see in order to perceive the constant stimulus of the world around them. Even though the realm of consciousness has given us spiritual direction, we must use our own abilities to hear and see our way through our earthly experiences. We are free to choose how we react to the stimuli around us.

As we are blessed with the power and freedom of choice, therefore, we can apply an attitude of gratitude or we can go negative, and wallow in the misfortunes that are a constant theme, a constant challenge in everyday life. Every human is given free will and is tested by the mere fact of their existence. Each of us is tested and it is the responsibility of the individual to realize his/her own autonomy and how it is best leveraged to maximize the experiences of our precious, limited time on Earth. Our universal call is to face our challenges with courage and gratitude so that we may evolve.

We are often taught that facing hardship requires us to think positively, stay calm, and to remain patient to help facilitate resolution. Yet, experiencing anger and frustration while encountering challenges is normal, especially in times of severe hardship, oppression, and injustice. Shutting down or regarding your feelings as invalid only leads to further suppression and does not allow one to effectively manage the natural flow of emotions. Running away from our emotional tides will not enable us to grow as people. We cannot control when these emotions surface, but we can control our reactions and how we choose to channel the energy arising from emotional responses. By understanding the manner in which people tend to react to stressors, we can embrace our challenges in a productive manner and with clearer eyes. The Qur'an speaks to many of these universal experiences, which I collectively refer to as the "Universal Laws of Human Nature." Here are a few specifics as mentioned in the Qur'an:

Attitude	Qur'an Verse Translation
Anxiety	Indeed, humans were created anxious. (al-Ma'arij, 70:19)
Grief and Sorrow	If negativity impacts him, he is in deep grief or sorrow. (al-Ma'arij, 70:20)
Stinginess	And if the good impacts him, he becomes stingy. (al-Ma'arij, 70:21)
Impulsivity	And humans are very impulsive. (al-Israa', 17:11)
Ungratefulness	Humans are ungrateful. (al-Israa', 17:67)
Desperation	And when adversity hits him, he is in despair. (al-Israa', 17:83)
Stinginess	Humans have always been stingy. (al-Israa', 17:100)
Injustice and Ignorance	Indeed he is unjust and ignorant. (al-Ahzab, 33:72)
Excessive Contentiousness	And human beings tend to be argumentative. (al-Kahf, 18:54)

If we take a deeper dive into these verses, we gain insight into some of the human truths embedded in the Qur'an. Specifically, verse 18:54 describes the human inclination toward argumentation as the most common of my aforementioned "Universal Laws of Human Nature." The Arabic word *jadala* is used in this particular verse to describe the English word "argumentative." The root word of *jadala* literally means "twisting a rope." Conceptually, a rope's component fibers continuously wrap around an invisible vertical line. The central vertical core is symbolic of a clear truth, a truth which we all know and recognize deep within ourselves. But, like the rope fibers that do not follow this vertical line directly, we too send our consciousness off in many directions instead of fully aligning ourselves fearlessly with what we know to be the truth. This "twisting" of words and ideas often serves to obfuscate the truth and otherwise mangle accord among people, causing strife instead of helping us align with our higher selves. Scoring points and winning arguments may seem like a victory until it is compared to the damage caused to relationships, our integrity, and ultimately, the truth.

The first three verses in the table above are taken from Surah al-Ma'arij. These verses describe some of the negative traits of raw human nature. They are followed, however, by an acknowledgement that those who strive to be in constant harmony with the universe will be rewarded with spiritual growth. So, we see that being able to master our human nature in order to find and follow our inner guidance will help us to better direct our consciousness, ultimately steering it towards the truth.

This inner guidance is our consciousness (Arabic: *rūḥ*), which leads us to the enlightened path. This consciousness can easily become overpowered by the many universal aspects of human nature not under control, thus a conflict within us begins to grow. While we are inherently *capable* of choosing only those actions that align with the purest way of being, it is easy to make choices that do not align with spiritual evolution. Even after we learn about that which is morally and spiritually ideal, the human tendency is to make excuses and to veer off a spiritually enlightened path, choosing instead to follow a superficial, materialistic path.

Fortunately, however, our consciousness informs us when we have deviated from the ideal path. If you take an action you know is wrong, you can feel the weight of a poor choice inside despite the excuses made to absolve the guilt. This "gut feeling," or conscience, is within us all and is described in Qur'anic verses 75:14-15 (Surah al-Qiyama): "Yes, Man against himself shall be insightful / although he may put forth his excuses." If we take a closer look at the Arabic, we see the word meaning "insightful." Interestingly, we have the same root word in Surah al-Insan (76:2) mentioned previously. In al-Insan, this word refers to the capacity for physical sight. Here in al-Qiyama, it refers more to internal vision, or the ability to perceive our emotional state. In order to remain in alignment with our highest potential, we must take advantage of the innate capacity to look within, an ability that is directly connected to the greater consciousness.

If we approach the world with a sense of humility and choose to utilize our capacity for love, compassion, and responsibility instead of merely our intellectual ability to rationalize, we can avoid making excuses that turn us away from the path of spiritual evolution. Oftentimes, we need to prevent our head from blocking our heart. Progress requires constant vigilance and a conscious decision to shift our awareness toward that which aligns with our spiritual goals. We can liken this journey to a walk through a dark house with many rooms. Equipped with a flashlight, we shine it where we would like to walk. If we shine it into a room filled with negativity, we will enter the space and become encompassed by sadness, anger, laziness, etc. If we shine it into a room filled with happiness and love, then we will be surrounded with positive energy. In our search through the dark rooms of the house, and more importantly, the unknown nooks in life, our feet follow the light and our energy flows where we choose to direct our attention. So, we must consciously choose to point our flashlight where we want to go. If we direct our attention toward negativity, the longer we leave our light on in this room, the more we inevitably continue to travel in this direction and the harder it will be to turn around. By the same token, when we deliberately head in a positive direction, we are surrounded by uplifting, supportive energy that distances or even helps to remedy our troubles.

Becoming aware of one's thoughts is the critical first step in addressing difficulties or hardships. Listening to our "inner voice" allows us to acknowledge the reality of our situation. It gives us the opportunity to push aside lingering negative thoughts, ideas, or perspectives, enabling us to embrace positive ones. Should we ignore this chance, a warning comes from Surah al-Shams:

1. And the soul and He who proportioned it.
2. And inspired it with its wickedness and its righteousness.
3. Successful is he who purifies it.
4. Failing is he who degrades it.

The above verses clearly state that either we purify our souls and improve ourselves, or we fall back into our default, unenlightened ways and fail to grow.

This applies to us both as individuals and to

our society as a whole. The famous verse in Surah al-Ra'ad (13:11) states, "God will not change the condition of folks until they change what's within themselves." Like the many bits of genetic material that make up the "drop" of Creation, our individual beings comprise our society. If we, as individuals, are faulty then how can the collective "us" expect to create something coherent and cohesive when we come together as a single community? Each of us has a responsibility, not just to our individual selves, but to humanity as well. It is incumbent upon each one of us to do our part, to be responsible, conscious, and to commit to the process of evolving our mind, body, and spirit. So, make a conscious effort to focus your awareness on the positive rooms in your spiritual house. Take deep breaths to allow your energy to flow in the desired direction, and commit to making meditation a part of your daily life. And do not forget the simple maxim: if you have a problem, you also have the solution. Let us take a moment to explore how in concrete terms.

Throughout my personal journey, I have to come to understand that the challenges we typically face in our lives are rarely the apparent challenge that appears before our eyes. Rather, the true challenge, the real problem we tend to face, is most often the manner in which we approach our challenges generally speaking. As humans we tend to oversimplify our identity, choosing to focus merely on the physical body that we view in the mirror. Unfortunately, we either forget, or ignore, the fact that we are a larger, more comprehensive manifestation of pure consciousness experienced by the present self, moment-by-moment. As such, we must learn in our limited time to manage our emotions and to evolve both our physical shell and our greater consciousness. So as an analogy, when your car breaks down, leaving you stranded by the roadside, it is common in the USA to call the American Automobile Association (AAA) for assistance. In this same manner, when seemingly intractable problems result in feelings of being stranded, instead of blindly reaching out for hopeful answers, there is a different "Triple A" that we can call upon to stimulate our sense of awareness: Accountability, Acceptance, and Appreciation.

We are thrust into these lives that are "given" to us, unique individuals each with a story, our successes lifting us up, our failures attempting to pull us down. In the first few chapters I have shared my life's journey and some of the lessons I have learned along the way. My hope is that these experiences, my lessons learned, act as a set of tools that others can use to navigate their challenges and tests in life. In teaching, I have always attempted to focus on the positive, to foster confidence and a "can-do" spirit in the minds of my students. In a classroom, everyone is expected to ultimately learn the same course information, but each individual student arrives on day one as just that, an individual. In mathematics, some students arrive with natural ability and ace tests straight away. For others, there may be a slog and the frustrations associated with it. Some will have ambition and motivation to spare while others will plan to just go through the motions in order to complete a required course. Each student will ultimately face the test at the end of the course and each will either succeed and move on, or, fail and have to consider their next steps. Tests in life are no different, and each of us must do our best to prepare for the many unknown tests that lie ahead.

Accountability

In short, accountability means taking responsibility for your actions and reactions. It requires a will to notice and keep track of your emotional experiences, flawed as they may be, and use this information to chart a course for change. It is easy to cast blame on others for the problems we experience in life, but true desire to improve oneself begins with accepting full responsibility for individual life choices. I once heard a preacher compare this process to being self-employed and striving to fix one's business. When you are the only one running the show, all decisions and opportunities point back at you. In other words, you are both the patient and the doctor, as well as your own nurse, pharmacist, physical therapist, and social worker. There is no one else to call on but yourself!

Establishing a heightened sense of

accountability in one's life is no small undertaking. Initiating huge systemic changes often require us to confront uncomfortable feelings. Although the process may result in unease, we need to understand that by acknowledging and working through the discomfort, we create the opportunity to fix or improve our situation. One method that can help a person to improve accountability is journaling to chronicle specific actions, reactions, and feelings. Of particular importance is to document emotionally charged situations such as when we lash out at a friend or say something unkind to a family member. These instances, while unpleasant to record, are important for future reflection and potential growth. Developing a habit of revisiting the entries well after the fact can assist in understanding the connections between our actions and the triggering situations. When we are capable of reading the journal as if it were a novel, dispassionately analyzing the situations described therein, we may begin to identify alternative (i.e. calmer, less rash) responses we can leverage in future situations.

In order for us to evolve, we must face our

faults head-on. The regret brought into focus by hindsight can be channeled into suppressing unwanted responses in the future. I truly believe that many people can make big, positive life changes if they keep a journal and use it habitually as a tool to improve themselves. To support your self-improvement efforts, try to surround yourself with friends and family that aim to do good in the world, and consider their actions as a mirror to reflect upon your own follies. Oftentimes, observing others can be the best guide for learning about yourself. Measure yourself against the evaluations you impose upon those you respect and admire. Use this comparison to identify and resolve your own personal shortcomings. Using self-reflection, jot notes detailing the triggers of your shortcomings and use these notes to develop behavioral frameworks and action plans to improve your behavior in times of stress.

Acceptance

A common misunderstanding of this word

suggests that one must sit back and accept whatever hardships come along without putting up a fight. True acceptance, however, is far from being resigned to fate, nor does acceptance imply one must be content with one's circumstances. Rather, acceptance is simply the ability to acknowledge a situation *as it is* in the present moment. At the same time, acceptance is not sitting back and letting life steamroll us or pass us by. Acceptance allows us to take stock of our surroundings *and to take appropriate action*. In contrast, there are two noticeably inappropriate, unhelpful alternative actions: dwelling on the past and worrying about the future. We cannot change the past, and we cannot tell what is to come. Disconnecting from the present moment creates an incapacitating anxiety, a trap deployed by the ego to keep us glued to old fears and memories of suffering.

An important aspect of acceptance is forgiveness. We can forgive the past by letting go of our suffering, starting from the oldest memories of our childhood up until the most recent injuries. We can forgive the future by letting go of our crippling concerns, choosing instead to channel our energy into preparation for positive scenarios we can imagine. We can also forgive ourselves and others for our personal limitations, whatever they may be. When we accept where we are in life, we can appreciate how far we have come and look forward to the journey ahead. Feelings of fear, failure, or inadequacy hold us captive while, conversely, we are freed when we foster acceptance and view life's challenges as opportunities to grow. Ultimately, we can free our minds to enjoy the challenges we face, because we can choose to view them as part of a process for achieving success.

Acceptance is a state of mind. It requires conditioning and conviction. If we remind ourselves that what has happened cannot be changed, we can focus on dealing with that which is within our control. If we can stay alert to our emotions, and remember that where awareness goes, energy flows, we can make our best choices to enhance the present moment and set ourselves up for success. If we believe that everything happens for a reason, we can keep our hearts open to experience the full potential of the goodness coming to us. The puzzle of "why" something happened may still be solved at a later date, and can be viewed as something we may actually look forward to. After all, the future holds innumerable unexpected but delightful surprises. While we wait for them, we can and should commit our energy to the situations at present. This acceptance of the present moment allows us to experience tranquility and contentment, right here in the "now."

Appreciation

Appreciation is relative. Our experience dictates what we know. A Maasai in the Kalahari and a Wall Street investor realize vastly different life experiences, but their individual capacities for appreciation are inherently the same. Appreciation comes from understanding and enjoying every thing and every moment for the value it brings. When we recognize the value in an experience, especially when it is challenging, a unique optimism takes root and flourishes in our soul. Appreciation encourages us to protect and celebrate that which is good, and transform that which is not. The dictum "when life gives you lemons, make lemonade" is the maximum case for embodying a sense of appreciation, as it is relatively easy to be appreciative when life is breezy, however, mettle is tested when times are tough and appreciation is not quite as easy. Challenge yourself.

Appreciation can be practiced at any moment, anywhere, and at any time. One easy way to incorporate moments of appreciation into your daily life would be to pause before meals in a moment of quiet reflection and gratitude. Imagine the journey of your food, simply, how it arrived. Perhaps its ingredients were purchased from a grocery store. The employees worked to make it available for purchase. Prior to that, a truck brought it from the distribution center. And before that, it was produced or packed in a kitchen, factory, or farm. Earlier still, the sun shined on the crops, ripening them. The weather and seasons orchestrated this seemingly miraculous yet incalculably frequent dance of sustenance. The universe organized the energy needed to regulate the Earth to enable the events leading to the meal. When we trace everything back to the Source, we tap into the greatest energy known to humankind. Truly, each one of us is connected to everyone and everything.

With appreciation in our hearts, we situate ourselves in a nexus of limitless gratitude. All possibilities open up to us, and the light of awareness is within sight. We stand ready and confident to face the tests of life.

5

ABRAHAM'S WAY

In a sense, the results of a human's spiritual testing is perhaps best illustrated by the understanding humans develop with respect to their own, personal, metaphysical reality. Coming to terms with reality is not an easy task. Day-to-day challenges are pressing and can cause seemingly never-ending amounts of cumulative stress that distract us from bigger-picture projects. But, because these issues are still not so big, it is possible to analyze poor behaviors/associations and work towards a solution that aims to improve daily life. Larger, more comprehensive challenges (educational, career, interpersonal, and so on), however, can certainly test our mettle in life more vigorously, upending plans, dissolving expectations, or causing anguish that can threaten our emotional and mental stability.

When faced with these broad issues, if we allow our minds to shift to the largest "problem domain" possible, we inevitably end up staring down the chasm of our very existence and questioning the existence of all that is. When we ponder the metaphysical space, the range of variables are not only incalculable but the available methods of understanding this space are increasingly murky and fraught with ambiguity, not to mention the opinions of billions. As such, many people prefer to navigate these wonderings in private. Many years ago, however, Abraham very publicly engaged in such a metaphysical test in his desire to identify the "Source" of God. Regardless of one's belief in the nature or even existence of God, Abraham's search for truth provides a valuable lesson in how we can use our innate human abilities to confront our own tests in life.

In the Qur'an we learn that Abraham's process of constantly evaluating the external world, testing the nature of everything around him, is the best example of a human using his abilities to arrive at an understanding of truth. According to the Qur'an, following "Abraham's Way" is one-third of the recipe for spiritual success: "And who is better in the undeniable law than he who submits himself wholly to God, and is a doer of good, and follows the way of Abraham the straight? And God has taken Abraham in harmony" (4:125). I have always stopped at this verse and wondered, why Abraham? If Muhammad is the Messenger of this book, why are we asked to follow someone else? Verse 123 of Surah al-Nahl explains why: "Then we inspired you, follow the way of Abraham, he who kept turning towards the truth in constant evaluation of what he witnessed" (16:123).

In my quest to learn what was so special about Abraham, I collected all the verses in the Qur'an about this prominent man. After intense research, I found that the root word of his name is "*barham*," meaning "the one who pays attention to what he sees." Surah al-Nahl further describes Abraham as "the archetype of alignment with God, who kept turning towards the truth in constant evaluation of what he witnessed, and he was not among those who associate partners with

God." We can also do well by following Abraham's example by turning toward the truth in constant *evaluation of* what we witness in the world around us. To understand the origins of this idea, let us examine the classic story of Abraham discovering the magnitude of God as told in Surah al-An'am. When Abraham said to his father Azar,

> "Do you take idols for gods? I see that you and your folk are clearly astray." (74) And thus we revealed to Abraham the realm of the heavens and the earth, that he would be one of those with certainty. (75) When the night fell over him, he saw a planet. He said, "This is my Lord." But when it set, he said, "I do not love those that set." (76) Then, when he saw the moon rising, he said, "This is my Lord." But when it set, he said, "If my Lord does not guide me, I will be one of the folk who go astray." (77) Then, when he saw the sun rising, he said, "This is my Lord, this is bigger." But when it set, he said, "O my people, I am innocent of your associating." (78) I have

directed my attention towards Him Who originated the heavens and the earth ... and I am not of those who associate partners with God." (79:74-79)

As we see in this story, Abraham looks first to a planet, then the moon, and then the sun in order to identify the most powerful, steadfast entity ruling mankind. Each time, he declares the celestial body to be his Lord. However, when he realizes the impermanence of each body, he eschews worshipping each, believing that if these objects are unable to maintain a constant presence then it is illogical for them to be divine. Eventually, he is left with the realization that nothing deserves his worship except "Him who originated the heavens and the earth" (6:79), the Ultimate Divine. Abraham came to realize, by looking both inward and outward, that the Lord is the originator and the Source of the existence of everything in the cosmos and beyond. The infinite light that illuminates both us as humans, the world surrounding all of humanity, and the immeasurable space beyond Earth is a light that finds true origin within each one of us.

We can apply this same "process of elimination" method to distill what is good, right, and true in our own lives, both in basic, daily life situations and also when attempting to answer the larger questions weighing on our spirits. Whether we are engaged in the banal decisions of everyday life, navigating workplace politics, or balancing extended family dynamics, we should strive for equilibrium and truth by evaluating all options carefully while constantly returning to foundational questions. What is the greater purpose at hand? From where did these options arise? In choosing a particular option, to where, ultimately, will the outcome lead? It is important not to be sidetracked by short term positives at the expense of longer term benefits of much greater importance. When we learn to see through the vacuous illusions of pop culture and the veiled lies they disseminate by way of advertisement (e.g. a bigger television or a faster car will lead to a happier existence), we can make life choices that align with our greater purpose and reason for being on this planet, choices that reflect our devotion to the pursuit of truth.

As the above verses describe, Abraham

noticed the sun and the moon provided light to the universe but disappeared after sunset and sunrise respectively. Yet, all the while, the internal light of knowing that came from within him did not disappear. He realized that the heavenly bodies were part of Creation, but not the Source of it. By implementing his own internal Socratic method, Abraham became "a leader of humanity" (2:124) and a wise man in full control of his intellectual capacity. We see Abraham's wisdom and reasoning skills in the story of his dialogue with the proud king (2:258). The king claimed that he was as powerful as God, stating that he could give people life, or, if he chose, take their life away. Abraham wisely chose not to argue this point as it could risk the king inflicting harm on one of his subjects simply to prove himself. Instead, Abraham challenged the king to a cosmic task: make the sun rise from the West. The king, of course, could not do it, proving his inferiority to the larger power that controls celestial bodies. Consequently, Abraham demonstrated his ability to leverage both his intuition (the king would feel cornered, have no logical retort to the challenge), and his reasoning about the natural forces that are governed by the permanent laws of the universe. In doing so, Abraham clearly demonstrated that, while powerful among men, the earthly king certainly did not rise to the level of God.

Abraham's signature story is the rejection of his ancestors' idolatry in favor of discovering a higher, more universal power. To be like Abraham and follow his methods and path to eternal internal peace, so too must we be critical of the teachings of our forefathers, or any institution claiming universal authority. Like Abraham, we must leverage our intellectual capacity and remain open to learning new ideas, new thoughts, in order to evolve our minds. An illuminating message is not always given to us, and sometimes, like Abraham, we must work for the truth through a critical examination of facts, assumptions, biases. We must also revisit the flawed stories we have been told over time and the tales we have told ourselves about the world. These stories and ideas can nest deep in our subconscious, preventing us from seeing the reality of our existence in the way a pair of fogged glasses prevents us from seeing the world around us with clarity. If we put forth the effort to search for truth, to deconstruct our thinking in a critical, immersive manner, we will be able to live in peace with a greater sense of truth and wisdom guiding our path in life.

Imagine a world where everyone committed themselves to seeking connection with, and gaining a true understanding of, the higher consciousness. Imagine yourself making this choice. The change that occurs in one individual can spread to the family, then to a community, then to an entire nation, and eventually the entire world. Never before has humanity been so ready to cease the senseless destruction of our ourselves and the planet. So, if you are ready to make a change not only for yourself but for the world community, then it is incumbent upon you to answer this call to higher consciousness.

6

THE STORY OF CREATION AND THE HUMAN FORMULA

Chapter One began with a memory of watching my cat Namira give birth to and care for her kittens, leading me to ponder the big questions about life, as a child. These questions have followed me around throughout the trials and tribulations of life, and my desire to unearth the truth embedded in these big questions remains unchanged to this day. One question, in specific, has garnered much of my attention over the years, namely: what does it mean to actually be human in a formulaic sense, and, given this humanity, what is the overarching purpose for human existence on the planet?

In the view of many Muslims, creation of humanity begins with the story of Adam and Eve as written in the Bible. A quasi-Biblical interpretation of the Qur'an arose in the 4th century AH (10th century AD), popularized by scholars associated with the "People of the Book" who shared the same theory of creation. Looking for proof in the Qur'an that supports a Judeo-Christian account of creation is a difficult task, however, since the Biblical Adam and Eve story is not written therein. Without direct qur'anic evidence for the validity of the aforementioned interpretation, I knew I must enlarge my circles of reference to other realms of research while retaining the Qur'an as the starting point.

For years, I have contemplated verse 29:20 in the Qur'an, which asks us to roam around the Earth observing how creation began. For the past ten years I have spent countless hours roaming the world of information, studying numerous scientific publications, including *Scientific American*, to achieve a better understanding of human evolution/creation from the scientific perspective. Reading scientific papers has opened my eyes to fascinating possibilities and truths about the human race, and expanded my understanding of foundational principles in theology. Specifically, the philosophical work of NASA physicist Tom Campell has been a wonderful discovery and resource. Campbell's massive, unifying theory (his TOE, or Theory of Everything) is in fact very similar to the creation story as described in the Qur'an. I think his flagship project, "My Big TOE" (MBT), should have been entitled "*Our* Big TOE," as it is the theory that many of us have been in search of for quite some time.

Reflecting on the story of the Qur'an during one of his MBT immersive workshops, Campbell said that life "is a game with a purpose." It is fascinating to me that Campbell's perspective on life finds him referring to it as a "game." In the Qur'an, life on Earth is essentially referred to as a simulation in preparation for a higher life that is meant to come in the future as referenced in verse 29:64: "The life of this world is nothing but distraction and game, and indeed the other home is the Life, if they only know."

Throughout his lectures and writings, Campbell is constantly reinforcing the idea that we should aim to reduce entropy in our lives (our simulations). This concept resonates well with me as I have always believed that when we bring order into our lives by reducing entropy, we are creating a sort of scaffold that can be leveraged in the future to build out the components of a successful life. As we work toward increasing order in our lives, I think it is important that we remain aware of life's purpose and to not become so completely immersed in this "game," all the while forgetting the actual goal of playing it in the first place. Much like a competitive sport, there are rules to follow in life in order to compete (i.e. live) fairly and ethically. The rules in this game of life are the challenges and tests each of us face as we travel along our life journey. It is important to remember that the "player" in this life is not the physical body, but the consciousness contained within. We play here to evolve, emotionally and spiritually, and to expand our consciousness as we gain wisdom from our experiences along the way.

In addition to Campbell's work, biologist Bruce Lipton's work exploring epigenetics, the link between mind and matter, offers an eye-opening investigation into the connections between the processes of the mind and the physical world. In *The Biology of Belief*, Lipton reveals that our cell membrane receptors act sort of like energy antennae, drawing power toward them. This same sort of transmission paradigm is mentioned numerous times in the Qur'an in a manner that suggests that human bodies are able to "receive information" from an external source.

Geologist Gregg Braden's many books such as *Human by Design* and *The Science of Self-Empowerment* have been highly influential in refining my thoughts about human creation from the qur'anic perspective. Scholars from a wide-range of scientific pursuits have contributed to broadening my understanding of how the stories in the Qur'an shed light on the physical realities that not only created our world but continue to shape it in the present. The similarities of function and form that exist between qur'anic descriptions and modern scientific discoveries are surprisingly numerous, making them impossible to exhaustively document in this thin volume. It amazes me how much cutting-edge modern science helps direct my attention to new insights pulled directly from the old, Arabic text of the Qur'an. Without keeping informed with scientific discoveries across many fields, I may not have been able to make these linguistic connections. This just goes to show how important it is to keep expanding one's frame of reference, on this or any subject.

Before we can understand the purpose of human life on earth, we must seek to understand where we come from. Whether by divine decree, intervention, or scientific accident, how did humans become… human? There is some genetic evidence pointing to the origin of modern humans, or, to be more specific, pointing to the origins of chromosome differentiations between apes and humans. At the 18th annual Los Angeles Conscious Life Expo, Gregg Braden presented "Unleashing the Power of the New," where he stated, "Many people are taught to believe that we are descendents of a former humanoid species such as the australopithecus or the neanderthals. Yes, we shared the earth with them and may have shared common ancestors, but we are not direct descendants of these species." Braden goes on to explain the research regarding human chromosome 7, the chromosome responsible for speech and complex language, and chromosome

2, which is responsible for complex emotions like sympathy, empathy, and compassion. Beyond emotional synthesis, chromosome 2 creates a class of neurons unique to humans called "rosehip neurons," which, according to Braden's citation of the August 2018 issue of *Nature*, is "what allows us to reach higher states of consciousness."

So, the next rational question is, therefore, where did chromosome 2 come from? An answer can be found in a paper from the Proceedings of the National Academy of Science (October 1991, vol. 88, pages 9051-9055), "Origin of human chromosome 2: An ancestral telomere-telomere fusion." It concludes that "the locus cloned in cosmids c8.1 and c29B is the relic of an ancient telomere-telomere fusion and marks the point at which two ancestral ape chromosomes fused to give rise to human chromosome 2." Stated in layman's terms, 200,000 years ago our ancestral hominids developed the capacity to feel and communicate beyond their immediate physical experiences, a consciousness expansion leading down the path to modern *Homo sapiens*.

The Qur'an points to this chromosomal

transformation in verse 15:29, referring to it as *nafkhat al-rūḥ*, the expansion of consciousness and awareness. This transformational process is linked to the creation of Adam, and Adam's subsequent empowerment by way of expanded intellectual capacity, resulting in the ability to communicate through language as further described in verse 2:31. But who is Adam? Who is this originator of man, as defined in the Judeo-Christian source material? In a departure from classical tafsir (the science of explaining the Qur'an), I posit that "Adam" is not the name of a single man who married a woman named Eve and from whom all humanity descended. Rather, "Adam" represents the overarching name of our entire species, *Homo sapiens sapiens*. The Arabic word *ādam* comes from the root word *a-d-m*, which means "mixed." In various verses, the Qur'an indicates two pre-existing entities, *ins* and *jinn*, that were combined to create *ādam*.

If we examine their qualities as described in the Qur'an, we see some interesting features. The *jinn* (created from *al-nār*, or "fire") are entities defined by their energy and power and correlate to what nowadays is popularly referred to as the "warrior gene." On the other hand, *ins* (created from *al-ṭīn*, or "clay") are entities recognizable by their easy-going characteristics. The fusion of these *jinn* and *ins* was accompanied by a merger of their energetic attributes as well, resulting in modern humans who manifest, to varying degrees on an individual level, elements of both. These manifestations of both *jinn* and *ins* can be seen readily in human behavior. For example, two individuals expressing high levels of *jinn* will oftentimes clash as each clambers to grab the reins of power in their dealings, whereas two individuals both expressing higher levels of *ins* may find themselves passive, stagnant or being conservative in action or motivation.

The development of rosehip neurons and the subsequent blossoming of consciousness within the human experience has given our species a unique opportunity: free will. Our physical bodies, primed and configured through the process of biological evolution, exist as avatars capable of connecting, both downloading and uploading, to the greater consciousness, a consciousness that is guiding the entire process of simulation (human existence) here on Earth.

Whether you believe this pivotal, evolutionary step results from an intentional effort by a universal energy force, or is the product of a remarkable biological accident, your abilities and responsibilities are the same. Whether your body carries more genes from the *jinn* or the *ins*, or whether your body carries more physical burdens or blessings, you are free to explore and deepen your consciousness at will regardless of your physical specificities.

Our physical body certainly impacts our perception and how we experience our time on earth, but if we can leverage our understanding of consciousness within a spiritual context, the particulars of physicality become almost irrelevant. Carrying this awareness in your heart frees you to make new choices every day, and enables you to determine which kind of human you want to be regardless of your cultural origins, socio-economic status, or the trivial happenings of quotidian life. If we take the initiative to fully engage our uniquely human capacity, to explore our own consciousness, then we stand the chance to maximize a joyous and successful existence on earth. We can recover from childhood traumas, reprogram our minds to eliminate bad habits, and heal all manner of physical and psychological ailments. We can set and achieve goals, and celebrate with gratitude both the milestones reached and the challenges conquered along the way. All it takes is tapping into our incredible wealth of consciousness, our human birthright, to push our souls down the path of evolution.

We all have personal abilities beyond our imaginations, latent but waiting for us to tap them, to take charge in order to actualize our dreams. As we see in Surah al-Sharh (30:94), "indeed, with great difficulty comes ease." No matter the trials you experience, be patient, work hard, and make sure to put your life in order, and a more enjoyable experience will eventually follow this hard work. It will help you stay focused and committed if you start with the little, tangible things: make your bed in the morning, sweep your floor, do your dishes. Put your physical spaces in order, and you will bring excellence to your surroundings. Excellence in your spirit is an inevitable consequence.

Reading the story of Creation in this way helped me to see the unity in consciousness, that we are all one and guided by the same Source. As we work toward reducing chaos in our own lives, we need to remain constantly aware that we are but a small part of a larger ecosystem of consciousness. In the process of growing and expanding as spiritual beings, we must be mindful to treat one another with love and compassion. Countenancing fear and driving unnecessary wedges between one another through excessive competition or comparison are forces that sap our creative energies, erode the wonderful gifts passed to us from our forebears, and inject entropy into our lives. Work for the collective good not only benefits those around us in the short-term, but maintains our momentum on the collective human journey to higher consciousness.

7

THE UNIVERSAL CALL

We are given this life, this simulation, and thrust headlong into this modern world of hyperspeed information, fluctuating human emotion, fears, doubts, unknowns, and confusion. Tossed like a wayward boat in a chaotic sea, we instinctively take the oars. In doing so, in engaging this life, we are implicitly tasked with becoming a fully formed human, becoming a member of a family, a society, an Earth-wide community. But is that enough? If this life is simply the testing ground for what is to come, then perhaps we should be playing the game differently. Perhaps we should be expanding our perspective beyond this physical realm, working through our tests to prepare ourselves for the bigger life ahead.

From the Islamic perspective, the example of Abraham provides us with a method for assessing the world around us, a template for how we can arrive at truth. Abraham's stories and techniques illuminate a path that each human on Earth can walk if they choose to answer their own, personal "Abrahamic call." Using meditation to connect to the higher forces in our universe, keenly observing the natural world for insights, and closely analyzing one's deeply-held convictions are not only time consuming but intellectually challenging tasks. Abraham's gnosis represents divine knowledge in its most primitive, yet most accessible form. His lack of dogma but methodical analysis of the world around him reveals that the attainment of spiritual enlightenment is a process accessible to anyone, anywhere and at any time. There are no prerequisites, no special gifts granted and no prophet designation required for a person to move their perspective to a higher spiritual awareness. However, this lack of structure and lack of authority means that the field of spiritual enlightenment is entirely open, a reality which can seem daunting at first. Is there no authoritative procedure, no accessible gateway that can help the faithful "see" the path, to make sense of how to behave in a world of seemingly unlimited moral dilemmas? Are there no tethers connecting to greater levels of spirituality which we can latch onto, to pull ourselves up to a higher consciousness one step at a time? Must we rely simply on the serendipity of pure inspiration if we are to ever achieve an "Abrahamic" sort of spirituality?

As mentioned in the previous chapter, Muhammad was asked by God to follow Abraham's way, to deliver the message in qur'anic verse 7:158: "Say, "O people, I am the Messenger of God to you all." God also instructed Muhammad to provide "clarity" to the world's people, essentially an additional layer of guidance to sit atop the revelations of earlier prophets as stated in verse 24:54: "It is only incumbent on the Messenger to deliver the Clarifying Message." I understand this "clarifying message" (i.e. the entirety of the Qur'an) as a reference book containing the fundamental knowledge for how humans can comport themselves on Earth, enabling them to align with the higher consciousness. This book of reference is timeless and, as humans evolve, it is incumbent upon us to use our intellect to understand the original language and how its meaning dovetails into our evolved, modern societies. Obviously, electricity, computers, cars, smartphones, and airplanes did not exist in the ancient world. Thoughtful readers of the Qur'an will understand that massive societal shifts resulting from the aforementioned technologies and the evolution of social mores and institutions over time require a deeper analysis of meaning for a text written in late antiquity. Furthermore the Qur'an, being over 1,500 years old, was revealed in a time when humanity's consciousness was in an infantile state.

Beyond the Qur'an's age and the need for contextualizing its meaning for the modern world, we must not forget the myriad authority figures (caliphs, emperors, imams) and governing structures throughout history that have co-opted the message of the Qur'an to serve both political and cultural interests. These powerful people and structures were, unfortunately, quite successful in recasting the language and meaning of the Qur'an in a manner that served authority but severely distorted the actual meaning of the original Arabic text. It is the fact that we have the original Arabic text, preserved through a tradition of memorization to ensure preservation, that makes the Qur'an such a useful source of guidance.

An etymological study of the original Arabic, through the use of various dictionaries, reveals many amazing and universal truths. In conducting these studies, it is fundamental to stick only to the Qur'an, avoiding the compromised translations of centuries past. Non-Arabic interpretations of the Qur'an, like all translated texts, are subject to misinterpretation for a number of reasons running the gamut between honest error and self-dealing. When reading translated copies of the Qur'an, the non-Arabic speaker has the herculean task of overcoming preconceived notions about the common meanings and modern interpretations of key Arabic words which often lack nuance and texture. For example, the Arabic word *Ṣalāt* is commonly thought to mean "prayer," whereas its actual meaning is "to put things in order, create harmony." These non-native speakers must be willing to consider broader meanings and definitions that come from a sound linguistic perspective. Native Arabic speakers must be willing to revisit the Qur'an with fresh eyes, ready to analyze the message of the Qur'an and eschew the common interpretive texts and pervasive cultural myths that have distorted the meaning of the Qur'an for centuries.

Islam, the religion of the Qur'an, is commonly defined as submission to God and belief in Muhammad as God's last prophet. However, in reality, the tenents of Islam are much broader and require merely belief in a single source of origin for all humans, acceptance of the fact of life after death, a commitment to being a good person, and a commitment to "put one's house in order" while on Earth. Islam is inclusive and no person on Earth is prevented from taking up practice regardless of race; demographics; or previous beliefs, creeds, thoughts or actions. At the same time, anyone acknowledging Islam as their modality of religious practice should embrace others' differences in order to see the humans behind the religious rituals, as verse 2:62 reminds us that all humans exist under one umbrella of God: "Those who believe, and those who are

Jewish, and the Christians, and the Sabeans—any who believe in God and the other Day, and act righteously—will have their reward with their Lord; they have nothing to fear, nor will they grieve." So, we should love and care for one another and aim to do good with our limited time on Earth; we are all in this together.

So, rulebook? Authoritative procedure? Dogma? Well, in a word, no. I posit that there is not a hard and fast structure prescribed in the Qur'an that dictates how humans are supposed to go about daily life to achieve spiritual enlightenment. However, what the Qur'an does provide is twofold. First, it is a book of wisdom that comprehensively describes human activity on Earth, enabling readers to get a bird's eye view of the often chaotic, confusing, and obfuscated reality in which we live. Second, it provides a philosophical template for how people should approach life, given the aforementioned chaos, in order to attain the highest level of spirituality. This recorded wisdom, and the example of how one should approach life, leads us back to Abraham.

So again, looking historically, Abraham's

spiritual explorations are the template for how man can "digest" the world around him: look inward to better understand how the external world operates. Abraham used his intellect and reasoning to deduce the nature of his existence, to better understand how the powerful forces around him function and how those forces are ordered. Abraham is able to intuit that, while massively important to daily existence, celestial bodies are not permanent and therefore are not the instantiating force of all that exists, and therefore none should not be revered as "God." Taken further, as Abraham realizes there is no apparent physical structure that can be labeled "God," he reasons that there must be a divine force, a "light within," that is the actual originator of the universe and hence worthy of praise, adoration, and worship. This reasoning is essentially a leaderless coup, a victory for mankind and his ability to leverage rational thought to make sense of the world instead of relying on the authority of charismatic leaders or brutal tyrants.

Following after Abraham and utilizing the message of the Qur'an, Muhammad finds himself in the unexpected role of leader, the bearer of a clarifying message to help steer the Muslim community away from idolatry and sin and back to the fundamentals of a moral and just life. Muhammad grows as a leader and leverages Abraham's example to help crystalize the concept of God. He encourages people to analyze the physical world around them, to look inward in order to logically determine how to live a healthy, just, and moral life. The pursuit of knowledge (both knowledge of the self and knowledge of one's environs) is critical in this journey of understanding both the physical and spiritual worlds and how they interact and inform one another.

In my own journey of attempting to resolve the glaring inconsistencies between the disparate artifacts of Islam (Qur'an, hadith, cultural interpretations, etc.), I have spent countless hours unearthing Muhammad, not only as a spiritual leader but as a historical figure. One of the best historical books I have read about his life and legacy is *The First Muslim: The Story of Muhammad* written by Lesley Hazleton. Apart from my disagreement with Hazleton's assertion that

Muhammad was the first Muslim (to be clear, it is my opinion that Abraham was the first, in the Qur'anic sense), I found that the book impeccably describes, in exceptionally researched detail, the intent and vision of Muhammad as he sought to elevate humans to a higher standard.

In Hazelton's book, we learn that Muhammad's mission was similiar to Abraham's in that they both aimed to establish a community based on moral principles, one that fosters intellectualism and ethical values. These values were practiced extensively by Prophet Muhammad as seen in numerous Qur'anic references documenting Muhammad's leadership by example. Described by his wife Aisha as the "walking Qur'an on earth", Muhammad spearheaded an ethical movement that focused on elevating human consciousness while simultaneously lifting people out of animalistic, barbaric lives, restoring their sense of dignity. His only real tools were the guidance contained within the Qur'an and his own behavior, a behavior meant to model morality and initiate a spiritual revival back to the path established by Abraham. For him, the raison d'être of Islam was to liberate mankind from the cage of its forefathers' idolatry, to resolve the custom of harmful practices, and to elimate obstacles masking the true purpose of humans on Earth. Adherents supplemented these objectives by undergoing a process of self-purification which enabled them to orient themselves toward a higher purpose. Muhammad's essential message was that the true purpose of humans was to realize that their potential could not be achieved by pursuing material ends, but only through a process of liberating themselves from Earth-bound, physical attachments.

Beyond spiritual leadership, Muhammad was also a natural educator from his first day of revelation and was inspired by the belief that the only sure-fire method to improve one's life was through a quality education. Amid the myriad responsibilities he assumed as Prophet, an enduring focus for Muhammad throughout his life was on freeing people from the bondage of others and delivering them into a just existence through the socially-levelling effects of education. As the last messenger in the Islamic tradition, Muhammad represents the last opportunity for humanity to hear God's direct message on the necessity of spiritual self-determination on Earth. As a dynamic and inspired torch-bearer, Muhammad provided leadership for a nascent movement needed to broadcast God's message and align people en masse toward a loftier goal.

Although much about the world's societies has changed in the years since Muhammad's passing, and science, technology, social systems, and common knowledge have evolved and expanded exponentially, the message and call to spiritual striving still resounds today. The ever-shrinking world and the ever-expanding availability of information have enabled people to connect more easily, frequently, and independently, and have allowed for highly nuanced intercultural dialogue and deeper understanding of the nature of humanity. Much like Abraham used his intellect to deduce the nature of reality, modern humans can use their intellect and the highly-refined treasures of society (science, technology, social systems) to lead themselves to a higher calling. With the guidance contained in the Qur'an already bestowed unto humanity, an external savior is no longer needed. What we need is the willingness to rise above the chaos of daily life, commit to inward-turning meditation on the higher aspects of our being, and cultivate our awareness of the nature of the universe, this sandbox of the universal power referred to as "God," "Allah," "Yahweh," and so on.

A Universal Call is a latent force in search of a conduit. It is a flame in search of dry kindling. The Qur'an itself is not the Universal Call. Belief in Muhammad as a messenger of God is not the Universal Call. The Universal Call, for me, is an invitation to connect to the lessons gleaned from reading the Qur'an and from understanding Muhammad's actions with respect to the qur'anic teachings. It is a summons to grow the abundant awareness an individual gains when they turn simultaneously inward and outward to the universe in order to connect to higher ideals, higher truths. In the words of Bruce Lipton, if your spiritual "Christmas tree" happens to be decorated with a different set of baubles than the "Muslim" ones hanging from mine, then it is no matter. Your Universal Call is simply drawing you to a deeper understanding of the core, unadulterated messages, and actions and teachings of the prophet (or ideas) delivering the faithful message that resonates best with you. Only a heartful exploration of your inner self and the Great Beyond will open the possibility of expanding your consciousness, your awareness of the fundamental nature of existence. Reaching outward using the innate capacities contained solely within the human heart gives every one of us the opportunity to direct our intuitive antennas to the greater universal truths, and connect to the guiding forces of all existence.

ABOUT THE AUTHOR

Fatima El-Hindi is a multidiscilinary educator, Qur'anic scholar, author and mother of six. Her educational background includes graduate degrees in physics, engineering and Islamic studies. As an educator, she established the Nas Learning Center (NLC) to teach Arabic as well as Qur'anic and Islamic studies from a scientifically and historically critical perspective to Muslim youth in Syracuse, New York. Aditionally, Mrs. El-Hindi has worked as an adjunct instructor in both engineering and mathematics at multiple colleges and universities in both New York and Arizona. El-Hindi was born and educated in Algeria, furthered her studies in Syracuse, New York and now splits her time between New York and Arizona. This is Mrs. El-Hindi's first book.

For more information about Fatima El-Hindi, visit her website at:

www.naslearningcenter.com/consciousness

Made in the USA
Columbia, SC
27 February 2024

32360384R00088